MASTERING A MUSEUM PLAN

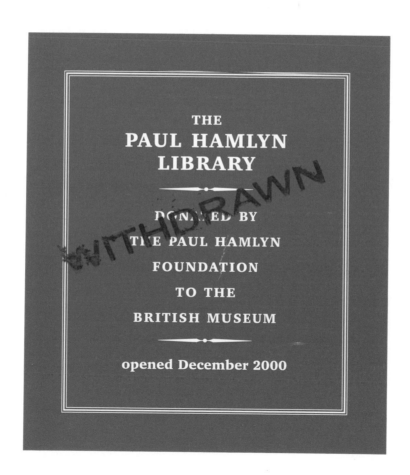

MASTERING A MUSEUM PLAN

STRATEGIES FOR EXHIBIT DEVELOPMENT

DIRK HOUTGRAAF

VANDA VITALI

WITH **PETER GALE**, EDITOR

. naturalis

. naturalis

Published by Naturalis, The National Museum of Natural History, The Netherlands,
Darwinweg 2, P.O. box 9517, 2300 RA Leiden, www.naturalis.nl

Distributed by AltaMira Press
A wholly owned subsidary of The Rowman & Littlefield Publishing Group, Inc.
4501 Forbes Boulevard, Suite 200
Lanham, MD 20706
1-800-462-6420
www.altamirapress.com

Estover Road
Plymouth PL6 7PY
United Kingdom

Library of Congress Cataloging-in-Publication Data
Houtgraaf, Dirk, 1959–
    Mastering a museum plan : strategies for exhibit development / Dirk Houtgraaf and
    Vanda Vitali.
        p. cm.
    ISBN-13: 978-90-73239-99-9 (pbk. : alk. paper)
    ISBN-10: 90-73239-99-0 (pbk. : alk. paper)
    1. Museum exhibits—Planning. 2. Museums—Management. I. Vitali, Vanda, 1949–
    II. Title.

AM151.H68 2008
069'.5--dc22

2007042054

Copy editor: Karen Jacobson
Project management: Betty L. Sedor, Christopher Coniglio and Fred Mooij
Design: STRIPE, Los Angeles
Printed in The Netherlands by Drukkerij Groen, Leiden
Images courtesy of Naturalis (Henk Caspers) and
the National Museum of Ethnology, Leiden

University of Southern California
International Museum Institute
IMI

Mastering a Museum Plan

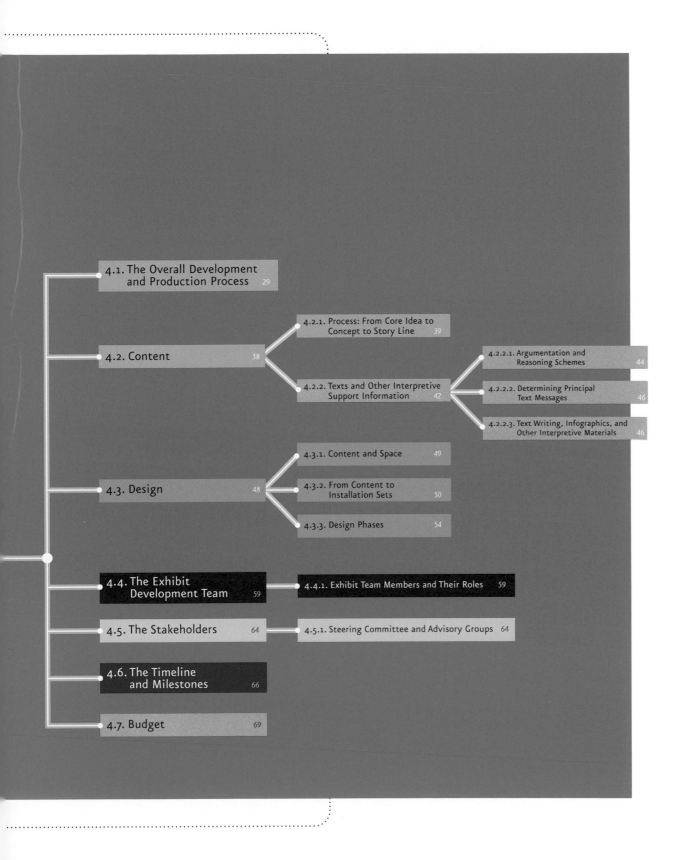

Preface

MASTERING A MUSEUM PLAN: STRATEGIES FOR EXHIBIT DEVELOPMENT looks at the process of developing a single museum display or, perhaps, the entire installation of a museum collection in new or renovated facilities. The book emphasizes the importance of establishing what a museum wants an exhibit to say and then considers how the institution might best organize or structure its overall knowledge, its resources, and several key aspects of the planning process in order to most effectively communicate its intended message and create a particular experience for its visitors.

In effect, this book is about making the most of exhibit planning by mastering essential parts of the process.

Mastering a Museum Plan results from the authors' many years of master planning for museum collection presentations and individual exhibitions. The methods highlighted in this publication have been arrived at with the help, collaboration, and team efforts of many colleagues at current and former institutions, whom the authors would like to acknowledge here.

The core of the methodology used at Naturalis, the National Museum of Natural History, Leiden, The Netherlands, was developed during the early 1990s, within the Naturalis team itself. This work built upon a methodology developed by Han Meeter and was enriched by contributions of many others, in particular Wim Gertenaar, Naturalis's design director at the time. In later years, others brought new contributions and refinements, especially Peter Zuure (production), Manon Laterveer and Hansjorg Ahrens (content), and Erik Jan Elderman (administration). They will recognize many of their ideas and approaches in this text. At the same time, *Mastering a Museum Plan* has had the full support of Drs. R.J.M. (Ronald) van Hengstum, general director, Naturalis.

For Vanda Vitali, the spirit of *Mastering a Museum Plan* has its roots in the logicist analysis of Jean-Claude Gardin, to whom Dr. Vitali is also grateful for having instilled in her an understanding of the need for any interpretation to have a well-developed method of reasoning. Collaboration with Pierre Royer, François Confino, and their consulting teams over many years has brought numerous refinements to the working method and specific components emphasized here. Lou Levine and Dan Rahimi, as well, clarified approaches to master planning that are singled out in this publication. The Natural History Museum of Los Angeles County Foundation is acknowledged for sponsoring the development of the infographic design for this publication.

Karen Jacobson's copyediting was masterful. Working from our rather complex PowerPoint presentations, designers Gail Swanlund and Jon Sueda of STRIPE developed an imaginative visual language for the infographics and text of this volume and also helped us clarify our work.

Betty Sedor managed the publication process with her usual dedication, tenacity, and effectiveness, while Fred Mooij and Christopher Coniglio supervised the production of this complex publication in an exceptionally efficient way.

To the above individuals, as well as to all those who read the text and offered comments, the authors are most grateful.

The support of the Mondriaan Foundation as well as the University of Southern California International Museum Institute, and its director Dr. Selma Holo, is gratefully acknowledged.

The Scope of This Publication and Its Audience

FOR VIRTUALLY EVERY MUSEUM, the display of its collection, or the creation of a temporary exhibit related to it, is a central, ongoing activity. *Mastering a Museum Plan* focuses on certain critical factors in the process of conceiving, defining, organizing, and realizing long- or short-term installations.

Indeed, the development and delivery of a museum display, regardless of its size or complexity, may vary from place to place and involve all sorts of people: staff from the museum's various departments; volunteers; trustees; donors and collectors; artists; representatives from local, regional, or national public organizations and governing bodies; consultants; and many others. Regardless of when and how they may be involved in the process, each will be interested in the content and message of a museum's intended display, why and how it is to be presented, and, ultimately, the effectiveness of the overall ensemble in public.

Mastering a Museum Plan therefore argues for the development of a particular strategy, involving certain essential components, for the realization of museum exhibits. This methodology stems from the authors' extensive involvement with long-term collection installations and temporary displays at large, encyclopedic museums. It is background that allows *Mastering a Museum Plan* to serve as an essential guide for the creation of new museum exhibits and the full realization of their intentions.

In addition, although the authors come from two different museum cultures, with different methods of approaching exhibit development, a recent collaboration allowed them to compare and contrast their particular approaches and methods of creating an exhibit. This has made the authors more aware of the need for museums to systematize important aspects of the exhibit-planning process. As a result, *Mastering a Museum Plan* has been developed for the international museums community.

Other books or sources outline the main steps that might be involved in the exhibit-planning process. They usually do not recognize, however, or sufficiently emphasize how important it is for a museum, when undertaking the creation of an exhibit, to organize its knowledge and resources in relation to the intended message, and to be sure to follow particular steps during the design and development of an installation.

Mastering a Museum Plan provides invaluable advice on organizing museum resources in order to define and then draw out essential or particular messages from research and collecting activities. This information can then be used more effectively within the overall context of certain critical aspects of the exhibit development process. Such a strategy can assist in the building of an installation scenario, including the design of the display materials, and increase a museum's capacity to communicate its message to different visitors while providing more informative and meaningful experiences to engage or activate their imaginations. These are especially important results for museums involved in the reconstruction of complex natural or cultural processes, which can be particularly challenging to present.

Mastering a Museum Plan will be of interest to museum professionals, exhibit designers, and architects, as well as to museum studies teachers and students—indeed, to anyone involved in creating and realizing successful visual communication. All readers will find that the book provides helpful insights into how one can organize resources, identify key ideas, and then create a more forceful and consequential public presentation or display.

The Essence and the Outline

1

MUSEUMS ARE COMMUNICATORS. Their essential "language" is primarily visual: objects, with their individual settings and overall scenography; moving and still images; labels and text panels; media presentations; and so on. These elements, and their overall effect, are vital visual components of a display. They come together in a gallery space to engage visitors in a particular message (perhaps a story, a concept, or extended information on a particular subject). The audience then "reads" the narrative by walking through the space and looking at the display, not necessarily moving along a strictly prescribed path.

The challenge, then, is to get the museum's message or intentions across, to translate them into a visual and spatial language that will engage the audience and communicate effectively. The consequence of that "translation" depends upon how well the collective information and resources *behind* the message have been structured and, in addition, how well certain aspects of the display, particularly its design and presentation, have been considered and carried out.

Indeed, a museum with complex, interrelated stories may want to summarize the knowledge of an entire field or discipline (for instance, a museum of natural history that wants to explain evolution or biodiversity). To do so, the museum should assemble and then structure its research findings and collection materials in such a way that the underlying rationale of a particular discipline also becomes evident when the desired information and supporting elements are eventually set out in a gallery display.

Equally consequential, the strategy of structuring a museum's resources can contribute to a visitor's recognition of the museum's many roles, particularly the complexity at the center of large, encyclopedic institutions.

To translate its knowledge and resources into a display, a museum will usually follow a plan, which may be highly developed or more informal. In all likelihood, a team composed of museum professionals from inside and outside the institution will be involved, along with certain work protocols or procedures. That process, and the intended message to be shared with the museum's audience, will ultimately reflect the museum's core body of information and holdings, and how it is organized, as well as how other critical components of the planning process, such as installation design and teamwork, have been realized.

Although the strategies emphasized in this book are directed particularly at exhibit planning, they are likely to be relevant for any type of systematic planning process that a museum might undertake, such as organizing live public programs, exhibitions on the Web, or other online presentations. The creation and realization of such projects also benefit from a well-structured organization of the museum's knowledge and collection resources, along with the use of other integrated planning strategies, described below.

At the same time, the strategies presented in *Mastering a Museum Plan* will also increase the effectiveness and relevance of a visit for the museum's many audiences, give further expression to its role, and generally increase public awareness and recognition of the museum's special place in its community and in the wider world.

As well, in **section 2,** below, *Mastering a Museum Plan* provides a philosophical foundation for the methodology and particular aspects of master planning that follow.

Why Structure and Plan?

2

THE NEED FOR A MUSEUM TO STRUCTURE its knowledge and collection resources, and to plan an installation that will engage visitors through spatial and visual experiences, stems from two sets of considerations: on the one hand, the challenges that museums face today and, on the other, a growing understanding of visitor learning in museums and how audiences absorb the various forms of information presented to them.

2.1   The Museum Challenge

The context in which museums exist today is constantly changing. The overall number of museums is still increasing, but attendance numbers are stagnating. The competition for visitors' leisure time is increasing while visitor expectations for a quality experience are rising. The growing sophistication of the visual culture and increase in the number of information sources are impacting the museum's role in the cultural landscape.

All this means that a museum must carefully consider its institutional strengths and resources, its possible roles locally and beyond, its competitive advantages, and its overall ambitions. From this process, a museum usually carves out a strategic plan that will focus activities and resources, both human and financial, on a prioritized set of goals to achieve the institution's long-term vision, mission, and values. This can include the development and promotion of the museum's "brand" in the marketplace, fund-raising activities, collection development, and an ongoing system of evaluation that will indicate, hopefully, that the right things are being done.

A museum is often committed to a broad public, even though an exhibit or program may be organized so that it attracts a specific audience or explores a particular interest. In all likelihood, the museum will want its activities to have wide and ongoing visitor appeal. This is especially true of displays that may be on view for a decade or even longer.

As well, a museum will usually want to be current and relevant. It exists in a world of constant change and knows that its audiences may have an awareness of or interest in developments in the museum's field. Disseminating information about new research and discoveries has become a necessary and expected aspect of a museum's role. This may be achieved through its exhibits and certainly through its lectures and public programs, its Web site, podcasts, or even blogs, each of which allows for a widespread sharing of new ideas and research with unprecedented immediacy.

Museums—particularly large institutions with broad, encyclopedic collections—usually employ representatives of various disciplines or specialties on staff or as consultants (in research, continuing and school education, programming, marketing, fund-raising, design, exhibit interpretation and technical expertise, security, etc.). In addition, there may be any number of stakeholders and authorities to consider, including local community interests, public regulators, various discipline-based organizations such as school systems, collectors, donors, and, in particular, a board of directors.

There is also a reputation to be maintained and protected. According to a 2001 survey on public trust conducted by the American Association of Museums, of various sources of information, museums are ranked ahead of books and television news as the most trusted source of information, valued particularly for the independence and objectivity of their information.

In order to meet all the above responsibilities and expectations, and remain true to its particular mission and objectives, a museum needs to pay particular attention to how it plans and presents its displays (in terms of content, design, and execution) and chooses the topics or stories it wishes to share with its visitors, particularly when developing longer-term exhibitions or displays.

2.2   The Audience Experience

Today most museums appreciate that they are no longer just object- or specimen-based organizations. It has become apparent that they must be idea-, experience-, and narrative-based institutions. Now, to a considerable extent, items in a collection are vehicles to help provide a context that allows a museum to share information and ideas in its field of activity, which may be historical or contemporary, artistic or scientific, eclectic or focused. At the same time, a collection can be used to provide relevant and meaningful visitor experiences: be they social, aesthetic, intellectual, contemplative, or entertaining, among other things. A story is an essential vehicle for effective communication.

The museum's audience can be as diverse as the ideas, experiences, and presentation elements that make up a display. Visitors may include many facets of the general public, who may be there for any number of reasons, as well as academics, educators, and collectors, to name just a few specific possibilities. To communicate with its many different visitors and address their varied tastes, motives, or interests, museums must take advantage of the growing body of research on learning and experience in their type of institution.

Indeed, the conceptual formulation of an exhibit's content and the overall structuring or logic of the desired learning processes and experiences intended for a diverse audience are important aspects of visitor education and appreciation. Learning theory indicates that knowledge and meaningful understanding are best encouraged through the presentation of overarching ideas and by making the audience aware of multiple or connected occurrences of particular events, happenings, or examples. At the same time, techniques that spark a visitor's imagination can be equally consequential.

It is for these reasons that museums need to care about the information that they present and the way it is communicated to their audiences.

To facilitate an understanding of the methods and protocols emphasized later in this book, **section 3,** which follows, provides an overview of the end results of one large museum's exhibit-planning process.

The Overall Result

3

WHEN A MUSEUM HAS MASTERED A PLAN for the installation of its galleries or a single exhibition, it should have a "content map" (which may represent a single gallery or an entire floor plan of the museum's galleries). This map consists of a floor plan onto which a sequence of themes is superimposed, with a preferred visitor route suggested as well. In addition, a series of sketches or images are developed to indicate the general character and major design components of each theme.

The creation of a "content map" and accompanying images represents the results of a planning process that goes from an idea to a full scenario and then into a three-dimensional visitor experience in the museum's gallery spaces.

To assist readers with their understanding of the planning process in general, the following section outlines the foundation and outcome of the installation at Naturalis, the National Museum of Natural History, Leiden, The Netherlands, in 1998.

Naturalis Museum

3.1   Naturalis

Naturalis started its development process for a new museum building and exhibits with a search for an "underlying core idea" for its exhibits that would have a strong, clear logic. As a result, the museum chose to focus on certain major processes in nature. The goal was to present nature's organization and workings and how its diversity was a result of those processes. The core idea, named "System Earth," was inspired by James Lovelock's Gaia model and was to show how our earth is a connected system.

The mission for the museum's exhibits, as defined at the time, was to demonstrate that "humankind is a part of a wonderful and complex system and must be a responsible part of that system." Naturalis chose, however, not to emphasize the threats to nature and possible human responsibility for them, but to focus instead on the mechanisms behind the natural system. The museum also wanted to demonstrate the simplicity of these fundamental systems and the extraordinary beauty and wonder that result from them. The exhibits had to create an inspiring and enjoyable experience for visitors.

The core idea, "System Earth," led to the development of a content structure represented by a division of galleries into two parts: exhibits on diversity and exhibits on natural processes. First, visitors would be presented with "diversity," including natural diversity through time and the beauty and variability of the earth today. The specimens presented would showcase the splendor and structure of nature. In the second part of their visit to the museum, visitors would enter "process" exhibits presented in three galleries, which focus on the "working machinery" of our earth. One exhibit would look at geological processes, another at life processes and their organization, and a third at the connectedness of the two previous processes in ecosystems.

To the side, Naturalis would add a more reflective gallery, in which different cultural visions of the organization of nature were shown in comparison with the scientific approach that the museum was presenting.

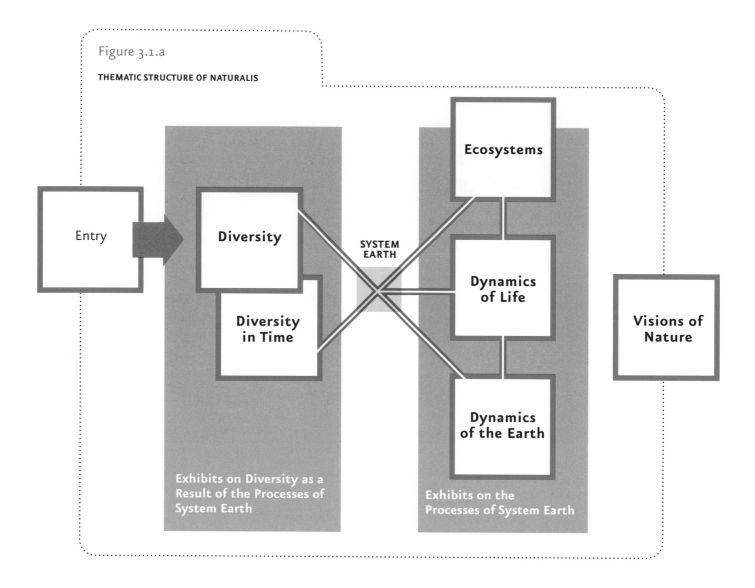

Figure 3.1.a

THEMATIC STRUCTURE OF NATURALIS

Entry

Diversity

Diversity in Time

SYSTEM EARTH

Ecosystems

Dynamics of Life

Dynamics of the Earth

Visions of Nature

Exhibits on Diversity as a Result of the Processes of System Earth

Exhibits on the Processes of System Earth

Figure 3.1.a shows the thematic structure of Naturalis. The development process for Naturalis began in the late 1980s. The content and its underlying logical structure were confirmed at an international workshop on the subject, held in Leiden in 1990. The creation of a new museum building, structured around the above concept, started in 1994. Naturalis opened this building and its galleries in 1998. "System Earth" continued to be the core idea, with the galleries explicating the logic of this system just as it was defined at the outset of the program.

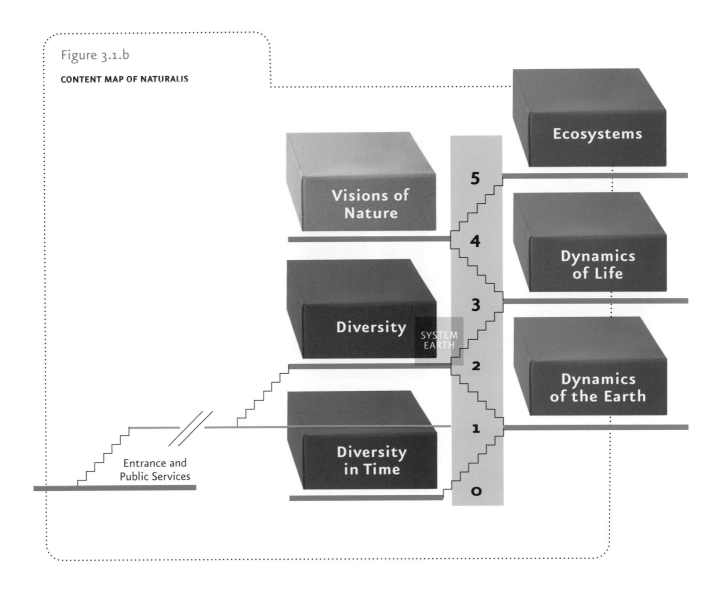

Figure 3.1.b

CONTENT MAP OF NATURALIS

Figure 3.1.b shows the "content map" of Naturalis when it opened.
Figures 3.1.c through **3.1.h** show the finished installation of the
exhibits in Naturalis's galleries.

The next part of the book, **section 4,** examines particularly
significant aspects of the planning process, including the development of
installation content, as well as important facets of the design process and
other production stages.

Figure 3.1.c **ENTRANCE TO THE GALLERIES**

Figures 3.1.c
through 3.1.h

EXHIBIT INSTALLATION

AT NATURALIS

Figure 3.1.d **DYNAMICS OF LIFE**

Figure 3.1.e **DYNAMICS OF THE EARTH**

Figure 3.1.f **DYNAMICS OF LIFE**

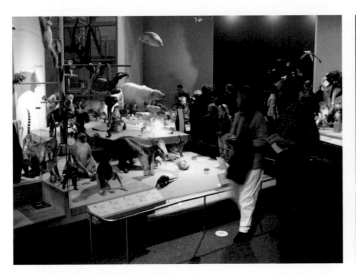

Figure 3.1.g **DIVERSITY**

Figure 3.1.h **DIVERSITY IN TIME**

Methodology: From Content to Form

4

The previous section of *Mastering a Museum Plan* allowed readers to see an example of a finished "content plan" for Naturalis, so that the following, more detailed discussion of its stages of development and particular ingredients could be appreciated in relation to specific proposals or finished installations.

4.1

The Overall Development and Production Process

For a museum to proceed from a general idea to a fully realized installation involves a process with four stages, along with six key ingredients that are part of those stages. These aspects of planning for a museum installation will be reviewed as a whole in this section.
A more detailed analysis of the six components of the process will then be presented in the subsections that follow.

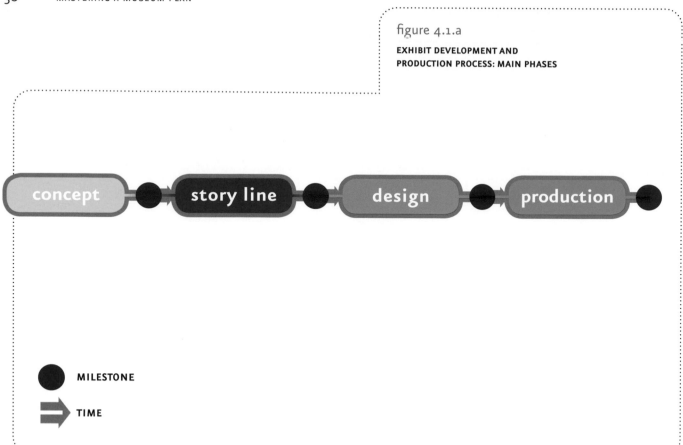

figure 4.1.a

**EXHIBIT DEVELOPMENT AND
PRODUCTION PROCESS: MAIN PHASES**

concept → story line → design → production

● MILESTONE

⇨ TIME

The overall process that moves an exhibit from a core idea for a single display or an entire museum gallery plan, through its design, fabrication, and installation, usually involves four stages, outlined in **figure 4.1.a.** It typically includes:

(1) the establishment of the **concept;**

(2) the creation of the **story line;**

(3) the development of the **design;** and

(4) the realization or **production** of the exhibit.

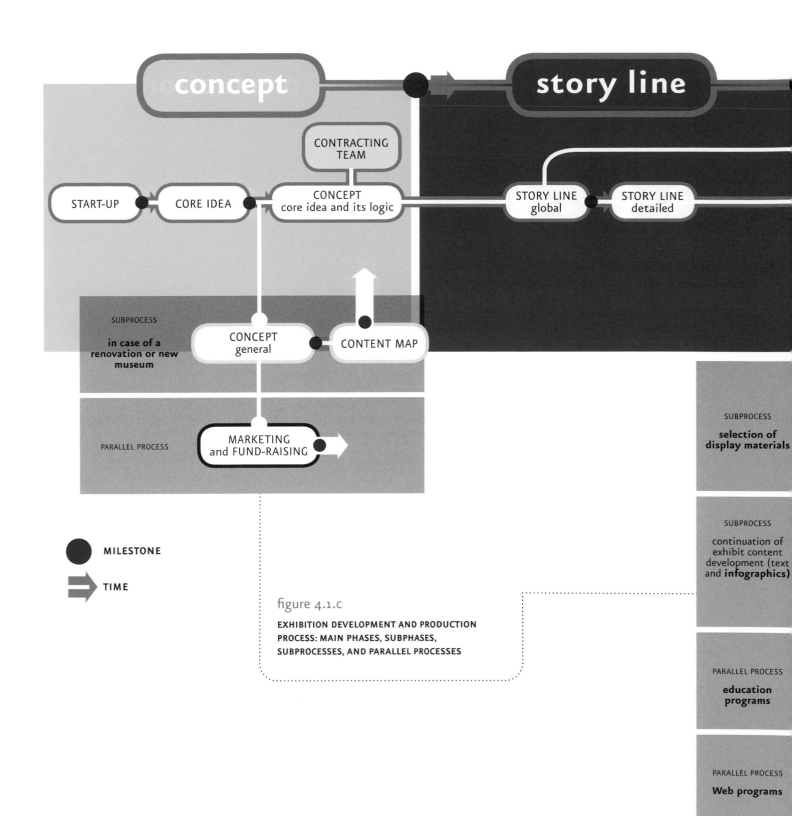

concept

story line

CONTRACTING
TEAM

START-UP

CORE IDEA

CONCEPT
core idea and its logic

STORY LINE
global

STORY LINE
detailed

SUBPROCESS

in case of a renovation or new museum

CONCEPT
general

CONTENT MAP

SUBPROCESS

selection of display materials

PARALLEL PROCESS

MARKETING
and FUND-RAISING

SUBPROCESS

continuation of exhibit content development (text and **infographics**)

● MILESTONE

➡ TIME

PARALLEL PROCESS

education programs

figure 4.1.c

EXHIBITION DEVELOPMENT AND PRODUCTION PROCESS: MAIN PHASES, SUBPHASES, SUBPROCESSES, AND PARALLEL PROCESSES

PARALLEL PROCESS

Web programs

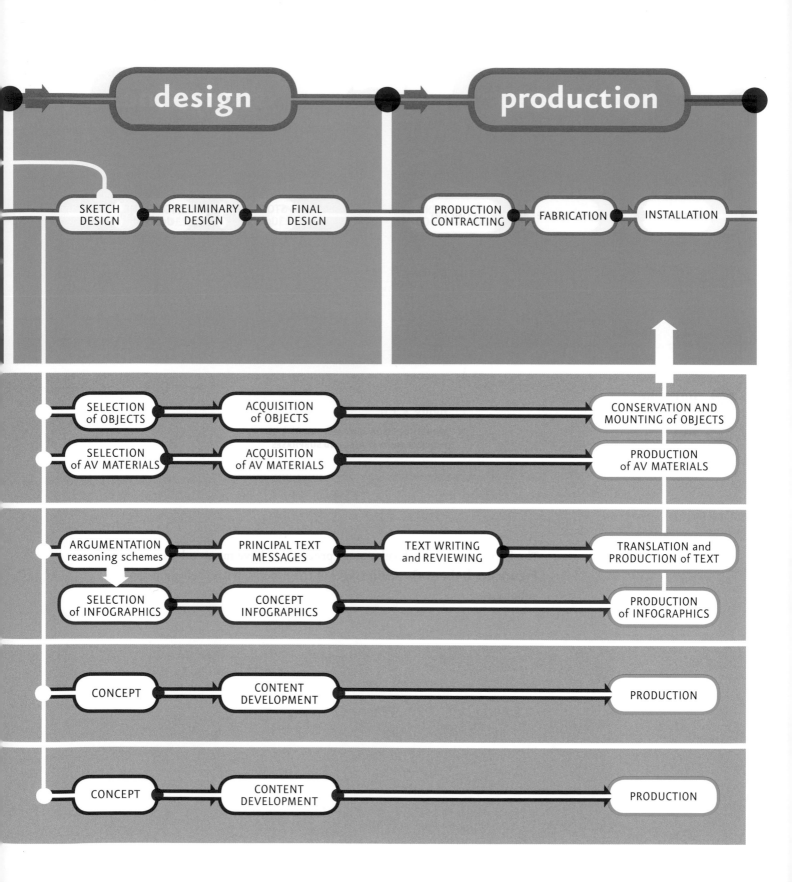

design

production

SKETCH DESIGN

PRELIMINARY DESIGN

FINAL DESIGN

PRODUCTION CONTRACTING

FABRICATION

INSTALLATION

SELECTION of OBJECTS

ACQUISITION of OBJECTS

CONSERVATION AND MOUNTING of OBJECTS

SELECTION of AV MATERIALS

ACQUISITION of AV MATERIALS

PRODUCTION of AV MATERIALS

ARGUMENTATION reasoning schemes

PRINCIPAL TEXT MESSAGES

TEXT WRITING and REVIEWING

TRANSLATION and PRODUCTION OF TEXT

SELECTION of INFOGRAPHICS

CONCEPT INFOGRAPHICS

PRODUCTION of INFOGRAPHICS

CONCEPT

CONTENT DEVELOPMENT

PRODUCTION

CONCEPT

CONTENT DEVELOPMENT

PRODUCTION

As well, each of the subphases of the overall development process may have its own subphases and parallel processes, which can advance in tandem before eventually leading to the production of all the components of an installation. **Figure 4.1.c** sets out this full process. A more detailed explanation of the process and its various deliverables is outlined in the appendix.

This process, in general, is established museum practice. What has not been a routine part of museum practice is the systematic organization of a museum's intellectual and material resources so as to facilitate their "translation" into three-dimensional stories. While recognized as an important aspect of the exhibit development process, the structuring of a museum's knowledge and collections in relation to their potential use in an installation is difficult. It demands considerable time and attention on the part of the organization to select and focus its material and intellectual choices (among the many possibilities that may exist at any point in time) in order to realize an exhibit's content, design, and, ultimately, its final, overall installation.

As a consequence, *Mastering a Museum Plan* emphasizes certain development stages in particular: the establishment of the exhibit concept and then its spatial story line, which leads to the development of the design and text components. This particular part of the process, which is isolated in **figure 4.1.d,** highlights the phases that are central to the realization of the content of the text in an effective exhibit.

Mastering a Museum Plan also focuses on six ingredients or components that it considers to be the methodological backbone of exhibit development as well as the master-planning process:

1. the knowledge and information that the museum wishes to transmit, referred to as the **content**;
2. the translation of the content into two- and three-dimensional **designs**;
3. the exhibit development **team**;
4. the **stakeholders**;
5. the **timeline**;
6. the **budget** needed to accomplish the project.

These six components create an integrated system essential for the realization of exhibits.

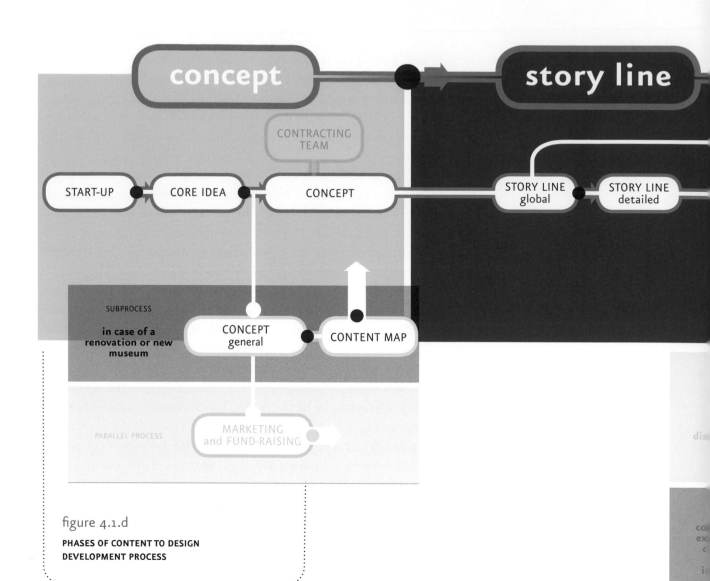

concept

story line

CONTRACTING
TEAM

START-UP CORE IDEA CONCEPT

STORY LINE
global

STORY LINE
detailed

SUBPROCESS

**in case of a
renovation or new
museum**

CONCEPT
general

CONTENT MAP

PARALLEL PROCESS

MARKETING
and FUND-RAISING

figure 4.1.d

**PHASES OF CONTENT TO DESIGN
DEVELOPMENT PROCESS**

MILESTONE

TIME

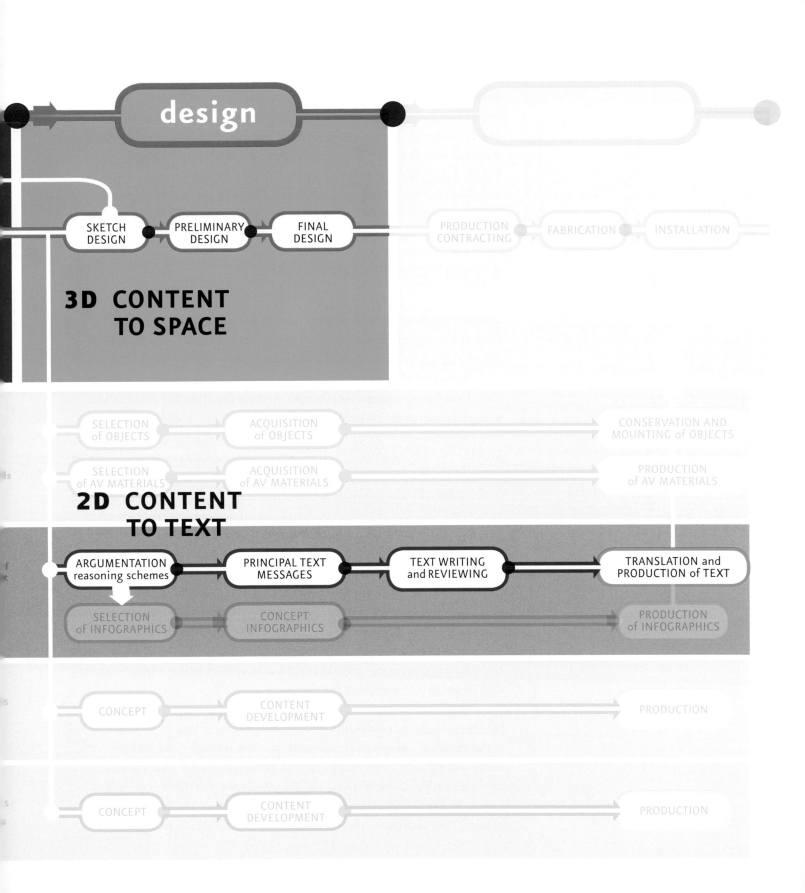

design

SKETCH DESIGN

PRELIMINARY DESIGN

FINAL DESIGN

PRODUCTION CONTRACTING

FABRICATION

INSTALLATION

3D CONTENT TO SPACE

SELECTION of OBJECTS

ACQUISITION of OBJECTS

CONSERVATION AND MOUNTING of OBJECTS

SELECTION of AV MATERIALS

ACQUISITION of AV MATERIALS

PRODUCTION of AV MATERIALS

2D CONTENT TO TEXT

ARGUMENTATION reasoning schemes

PRINCIPAL TEXT MESSAGES

TEXT WRITING and REVIEWING

TRANSLATION and PRODUCTION of TEXT

SELECTION of INFOGRAPHICS

CONCEPT INFOGRAPHICS

PRODUCTION of INFOGRAPHICS

CONCEPT

CONTENT DEVELOPMENT

PRODUCTION

CONCEPT

CONTENT DEVELOPMENT

PRODUCTION

Exhibit planning will possibly include other elements or components, such as security, retail connections, or project evaluation, as well as the development of marketing or fund-raising plans. The opening and maintenance of an exhibit will require additional considerations (see **figure 4.1.c**). However, the six items listed above are essential to the installation development process itself. They are examined in greater detail in the following sections.

4.2   Content

Today every museum is concerned about the content of its exhibits, from their capacity to adequately present the museum's core mission to the effectiveness of the stories told in individual displays or the details of each text label. If a museum is to properly manage or address this understandable concern, an effective structuring of its intellectual and material content is essential. It is vital, for example, if the museum is to maximize the use of its assets, modify displays in the future, and, as well, provide visitors with the fullest possible understanding or appreciation of its installations.

Nevertheless, many museum exhibits do not have a strong content structure. This can be true of both individual displays and the overall installation of the institution's galleries. Most museums offer a patchwork of exhibit themes, which often function at several different conceptual levels. The reasons are frequently historical: most museum displays were developed over time and reflect different ideas, practices, and points of view. This makes it difficult for an institution to remain consistent when presenting knowledge, whatever the source, within and throughout all its exhibits. Again, an ordered structuring of the museum's intellectual and collection resources can greatly facilitate the effort to provide a consistent and meaningful experience for visitors.

This section outlines an approach to constructing a strong intellectual and narrative structure throughout a museum. In effect, it is the museum's essence translated into a core concept, which then resonates through thematically linked galleries to individual thematic modules within a single space. Within all these areas there must be a logical and coherent clustering of information units (stories as well as objects). The approach described below allows a museum to map the domain of its knowledge and material resources and communicate their essence to the many different audiences that it may attract.

4.2.1 Process: From Core Idea to Concept to Story Line

The development of the content for an exhibition or museum-wide installation will start with a core idea. An exhibition's core idea may come from any number of sources and reflect the strengths of the museum's collection, its research activities, and its interests.

Nevertheless, the core idea that is subsequently adopted must be consistent with the museum's mission, its collections, and its intellectual activities. For instance, different natural history museums may have different core ideas to communicate—the public's responsibility for natural and/or cultural domains, an understanding of fundamental earth processes or evolutionary processes, biodiversity, and so on. Having a clearly articulated core idea gives a museum an intellectual context or framework, which then serves as a guide to the content of individual exhibits, galleries, and other programming activities. Identifying and then adhering to the core idea is not easy and requires a great deal of strategic thinking and planning. However, in order to avoid inconsistencies during the planning process, or visitor confusion later, the core idea, once established, should not be readily changed.

Once the core idea is defined, its components need to be elaborated and the logic of their "connectedness" determined and explained. This process of providing the core idea with an underlying logic produces the concept.

While many museum practitioners might express the concept and its logic in a text-based format, it is strongly suggested here that it also be set out as a flow diagram (see below). A schematic, figurative structure is more rigorous and unforgiving in its logic than a text-based format. Defining an underlying structure will then allow further work to sustain and expand on the same logic and avoid content inconsistency. As well, a schematic construct is much easier to translate into space and spatial relationships.

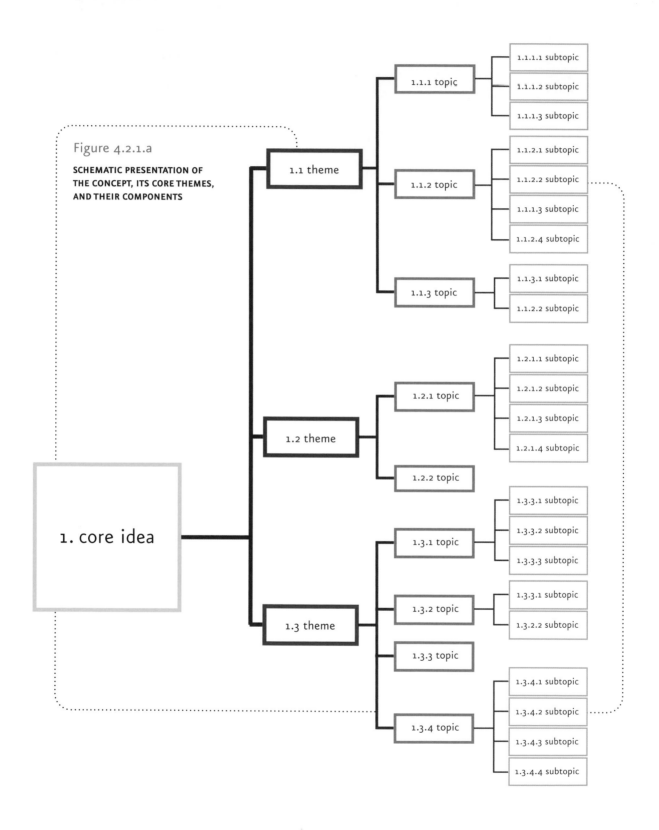

Figure 4.2.1.a

SCHEMATIC PRESENTATION OF THE CONCEPT, ITS CORE THEMES, AND THEIR COMPONENTS

This is a time-consuming phase of the planning process. If this phase is properly carried out, however, and a strong schematic structure is developed, then the rest of the process is set on solid ground.

Figure 4.2.1.a is a schematic representation of a concept, which consists of a core idea and its underlying logical structure of themes, topics, and subtopics. **Figure 4.2.1.b** represents a grouping of the components into logically aligned modules of presentation. While these modules are not directly linked to a space, there is the underlying implication that they would become thematic spatial groupings.

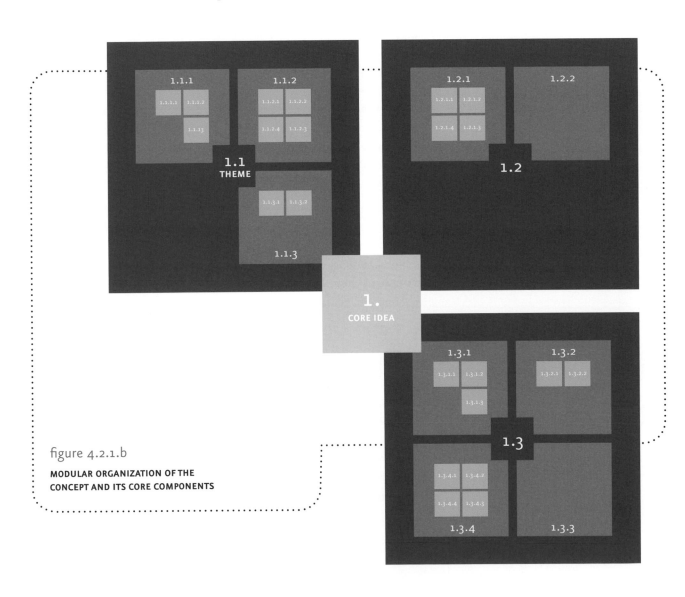

figure 4.2.1.b

MODULAR ORGANIZATION OF THE CONCEPT AND ITS CORE COMPONENTS

Therefore, this modular organization is essential to facilitate a later translation of content into space. Working models may also be developed to explicate the logical structure of the components.

The organization of a concept and its core components is followed by the development of a **story line**. This is a phase that requires research and a preliminary selection of key content examples, including collection objects or specimens as well as relevant support materials (infographics, video elements, games, etc.) not in the collection. This stage should include descriptions and sketches, if needed and possible, of the potential outcome. It is this outline that provides the museum and the exhibit designer with indications of possible or best methods for capturing and communicating the essence of a story.

When developing the central idea for displays throughout a museum, the story line would be a global one, with only the key components articulated textually. When dealing with a single exhibit or space, a more detailed story line is developed. Both global and detailed story lines require considerable writing time and should be comprehensive. **Figure 4.2.1.c** offers a template for composing a story line component for a single thematic module.

The development of a story line leads to two processes, which stem from it: the preparation of supporting texts, labels, and other information, which will be addressed in the following section (**4.2.2**), and the development of the design and its various components, addressed in **section 4.3** below.

4.2.2 Texts and Other Interpretive Support Information

The writing of supporting texts, labels, and other interpretive information, such as video segments or infographics, is not as straightforward a process as it is often imagined to be. It involves the development of the content argument and principal messages, as well as the writing of texts and other interpretive material, and is very closely linked to the overall development of the content and design of an installation.

figure 4.2.1.c

**TEMPLATE FOR A STORY LINE ELEMENT
FOR A SINGLE THEMATIC MODULE**

topic number	topic	knowledge, facts, insights	display ideas and options
1.1.1	Title and main content of the topic	Description of the topic, including essential information and, if necessary, drawings and sketches.	• Suggestions for expressing design. • Suggestions for objects, AV, etc.
Subtopic number		The description can be further explicated through subtopics and bullet points.	

4.2.2.1   Argumentation and Reasoning Schemes

Building the content for each part of a concept includes a careful articulation of the components required to express the concept in a coherent, reasoned format in the exhibit. The process of building the basic argumentation or reasoning scheme for a concept is particularly important when describing complex social, historical, creative, or scientific processes. It also assures that the experts who supply or contribute to this information (curators or guest curators in most cases) and the exhibit content developers, as well as the designers, educators, and other involved parties who might provide or use the content, will have a common understanding of the message as it is being developed. This helps to ensure that the message is delivered effectively by everyone who must eventually explain or use the display.

The principal objective for setting out the argumentation for any scheme is to see if the underlying insights into its content are thoroughly understood. If a reasoning scheme is well built, it can be verified by those with the necessary expertise and, eventually, enhance understanding of the content by the museum staff, its stakeholders, and its visitors. It accommodates questions such as "Is this how it works?" or "Where is this wrong?" A reasoning scheme is a valuable instrument to assure the clarity of the content. It serves as a starting point for drafting installation texts and for checking those draft texts.

The development of a content argumentation or reasoning scheme is a very difficult task. A reasoning scheme is often misinterpreted as the logical structure for text panels or as a way of structuring text elements, which in fact it is not. It is only the basis upon which the text is to be written.

A reasoning scheme is best expressed in a hierarchical setup (see **fig. 4.2.2.1.a**). Each major statement is presented as a separate bullet point. Every underlying reasoning element, or building block, is indented. Every indented element supports the major line under which it is located and can serve as a platform upon which a reasoning step or a technical explanation can be built. Reasoning can be expressed in various ways (e.g., fact . . . due to . . ., caused by . . . ; if . . . then, . . . else. . . ; as long as . . . then, . . . else. . . , etc.).

figure 4.2.2.1.a
REASONING-SCHEME TEMPLATE

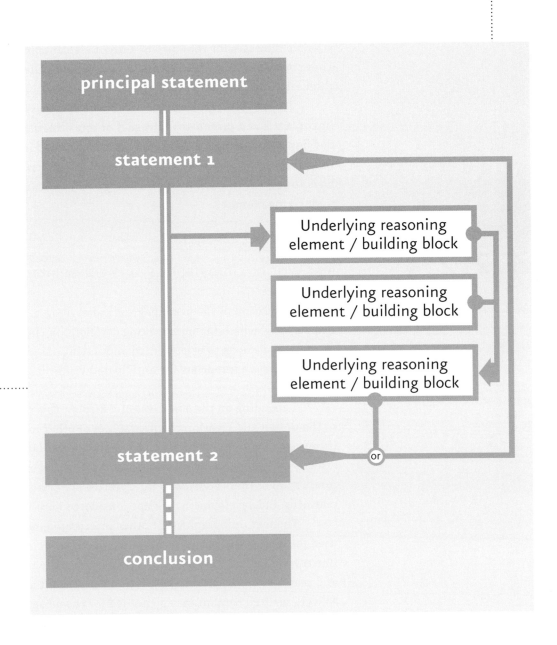

4.2.2.2   Determining Principal Text Messages

Once the overall argument for each display and its components is defined, the development of text messages follows. This phase involves determining the principal message, secondary messages, and other possible messages for the various content elements (see **fig. 4.2.2.2.a**). These messages then become the basis for writing the installation texts themselves (see below).

This approach to the development of text messages is particularly important when presenting bilingual or multilingual texts, or when developing traveling exhibits. Messages articulated in this way help those who did not participate directly in the development of the exhibit, or who have to present the text in another language, to clearly understand the underlying premises.

4.2.2.3   Text Writing, Infographics, and Other Interpretive Materials

The confirmation of the principal text messages (4.2.2.2) leads to actual text writing, which includes making decisions on the degree of detail in the various texts to be presented and setting out that information in different ways appropriate for anticipated visitor learning styles and interests.

Depending on the objectives of a display, this phase can also lead to the design and creation of infographics or other interpretive materials (films, cartoons, etc.), which may be more appropriate devices for effectively communicating principal messages. The creation, design, and production of these additional interpretive materials, which also require planning and development, are not considered here.

The text, infographics, or other interpretive means may then be used for information panels, extended information labels, object labels, or illustrative tools. Interpretive planners often write the information texts and may also advise on other aspects of the content and its development. As well, written content may be needed for the museum's publicity or promotional activities, donor development, Web site, or related programming activities.

Concise and clear writing is very helpful. Brevity, whenever possible, will usually benefit the communication of a message or story.

figure 4.2.2.2.a
TEMPLATE FOR DEVELOPMENT OF TEXT MESSAGES

Identity of the module

MODULE NUMBER	
SHORT DESCRIPTION OF THE MODULE CONTENT	
DESCRIPTION OF OBJECTS AND AV ELEMENTS	

Text messages for the module

	KEY TEXT MESSAGES	NUMBER OF WORDS	TEXT MESSAGES OF SECONDARY IMPORTANCE	NUMBER OF WORDS	TEXT MESSAGES OF TERTIARY IMPORTANCE	NUMBER OF WORDS
1.	Description of key information					
2.	••••					
3.	••••					
4.	••••					
	TOTAL NUMBER OF WORDS					

The core message should be expressed as directly as possible. It is helpful if the conclusion is presented up front, followed by the reasoning or explanation, preferably in the form of a story. Ideally the title should contain the principal message, in a more or less catchy or memorable one-liner. In other words, text titles should contain the essence of a display's contents. Having a specific, overall writing style can be very helpful for the consistency of the museum's communication with the public and for strengthening the museum's brand. Naturalis, for example, has developed a specific writing style and "tone" for all its written information.

The developed texts are carefully reviewed from a number of perspectives: scientific accuracy, educational validity, writing style, voice, copyediting, and so on. The result of this review process and subsequent corrections is a text that is accurate and generally agreed upon and that encompasses all the textual components of an exhibit so that they can be cross-referenced to avoid repetition before being printed.

At Naturalis, all texts are examined by a reviewing committee in a one- to two-week time period for complete batches of text. The same committee can be responsible for reading the exhibit texts as well as all marketing and communication material.

A community consultations advisory group (see below) may also be very useful in providing input at this point and help the museum steer clear of unintentional misstatements.

4.3   Design

Today more than ever, visitors judge a museum by the quality of the visual presentations they encounter. What can make a museum experience significant or memorable may be the overall "look" of the installation spaces, as well as the content of the displays and the design of the scenography, texts, lighting, audiovisuals, and other complementary components. These are the elements of the communication language that characterizes modern exhibit presentation.

While the sets or display backdrops, lighting, audiovisual effects, and other installation features are usually perceived as the principal aspects of design, the spatial organization and overall structuring of the galleries and the placement of the various components on display are essential to the effective communication of the content. This is where content meets design, where they must logically and visually connect and convey the museum's intended messages or experiences. The quality and consequence of a visit are very much influenced by the overall spatial organization of the content, as much as by the scenography, lighting, texts, and audiovisual support for the individual displays.

Museum displays are most effective when content and design are closely related, with design being a function of the narrative and the accompanying objects on display. Structuring the content and organizing the design process are particularly important when dealing with designers from outside the museum. This is frequently the case today, as designers are often engaged through a "request for proposal" (RFP), in which the museum must carefully and thoroughly articulate the details of the story line and content that it has developed and expects to communicate.

The next section of *Mastering a Museum Plan* addresses the spatial organization of display content, both throughout the museum and within a single exhibit or gallery space.

4.3.1   Content and Space

Once work on the content of an installation has established the substance of an overall concept—including its core display elements, their logical organization, and the resulting story line—there is a need to "translate" the developed scenario into a visitor experience. This might involve a single exhibit or the entire museum. A properly translated scenario with a sequence and hierarchy of encounters helps an audience to "read" the museum's stories throughout the galleries in such a way that they can take greater advantage of the various offerings and experiences of a visit.

For example, a museum visit begins with an entry space that caters to the arrival experience itself, providing reception information and a degree of release from pent-up emotions for weary or excited visitors. This is a transition area where visitors come in from the street and get ready for the museum experience.

Then, visitors might enter a general orientation space, where iconic items and other means of communication and animation, such as projection of key research or collection activities, would introduce the museum, its collections, its main themes and, perhaps, various professional responsibilities. In effect, this area should hint at the underlying structure and content of the intellectual and material resources that will inform the rest of the institution's displays.

As they move on, visitors would encounter more specific, theme-oriented spaces, each of which presents one of the main ideas or stories that the museum has decided to use in order to characterize significant aspects of its collections and intellectual resources. These spaces might include a cluster of exhibits or displays in which a particular theme is explored more fully and visitors might discover links to other display modules.

Figure 4.3.1.a presents a schematized, spatial organization of visitor experience as it might occur in a museum. There would be various ways of creating or realizing this arrangement, given the communication strategies that might be used and an individual museum's desire to create particular or overall experiences for its audiences. With already established buildings, there may be less flexibility to create new visitor pathways. What is important to note is that the content and spatial relationships of thematic modules established during the content development phase still remain the same. The general nature of the approach described here is thus valid for any museum.

4.3.2   From Content to Installation Sets

Based on the developed story line, the principal thematic content modules are "placed" in the main spatial units, followed by the development of three-dimensional "sets." The placement of sets representing thematic units again follows a "map" similar to that of **figure 4.3.1.a** but with a somewhat different focus. This translation of the display content into sets follows the model shown in **figure 4.3.2.a.**

The set design needs to express the underlying concept that makes up the topic being treated (or the process that is being observed). This would include a series of logically connected explanations that arise from the concept, as well as the manifestations of this concept. For instance, let us say that the "concept" is the way planet Earth is physically structured. One "explanation" may relate to the movement of the tectonic plates because of endogenous forces, and the manifestation of this phenomenon is through floating and colliding continents, resulting in earthquakes, volcanoes, and so on. The set, then, needs to address these three levels of intellectual structure—that is, concept, explanation, and manifestation.

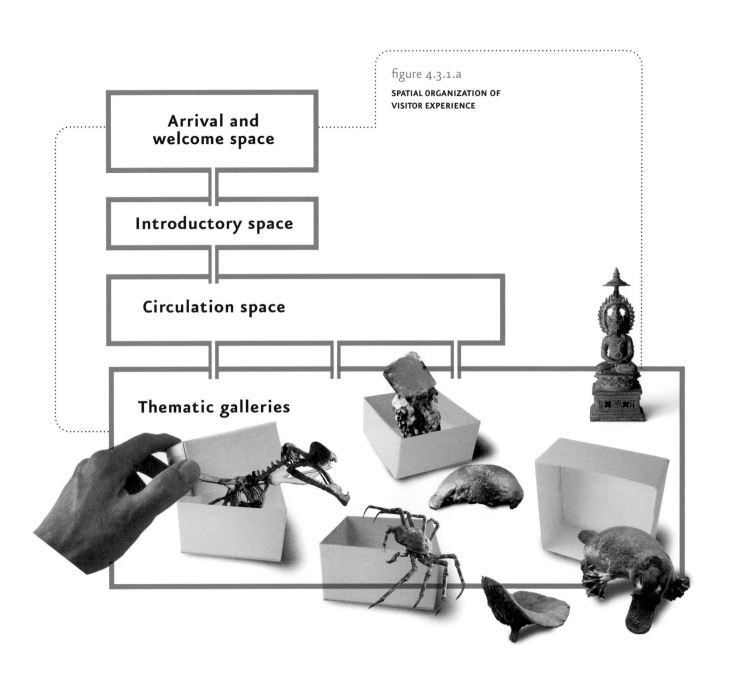

figure 4.3.1.a

SPATIAL ORGANIZATION OF VISITOR EXPERIENCE

Arrival and welcome space

Introductory space

Circulation space

Thematic galleries

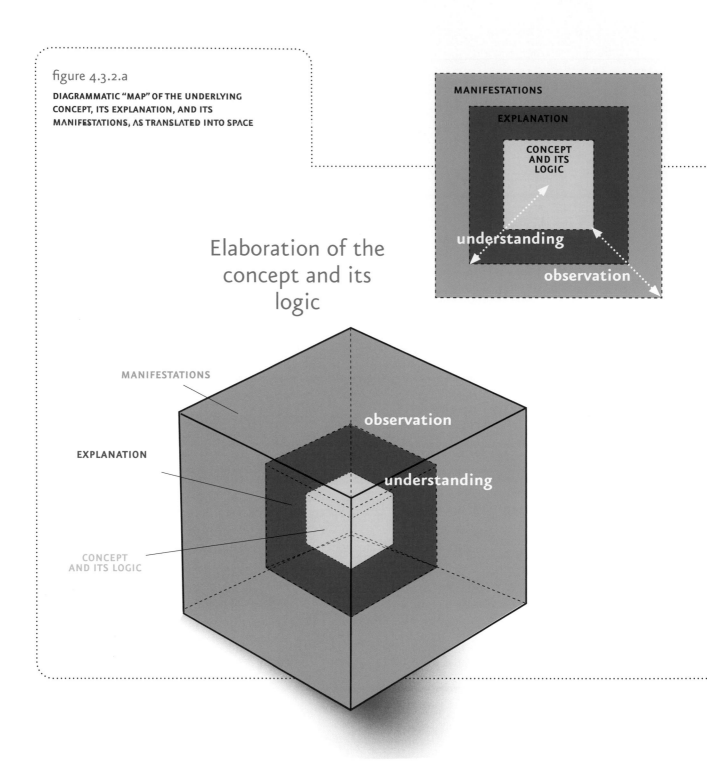

figure 4.3.2.a

DIAGRAMMATIC "MAP" OF THE UNDERLYING
CONCEPT, ITS EXPLANATION, AND ITS
MANIFESTATIONS, AS TRANSLATED INTO SPACE

MANIFESTATIONS

EXPLANATION

CONCEPT
AND ITS
LOGIC

understanding

observation

Elaboration of the
concept and its
logic

MANIFESTATIONS

EXPLANATION

CONCEPT
AND ITS LOGIC

observation

understanding

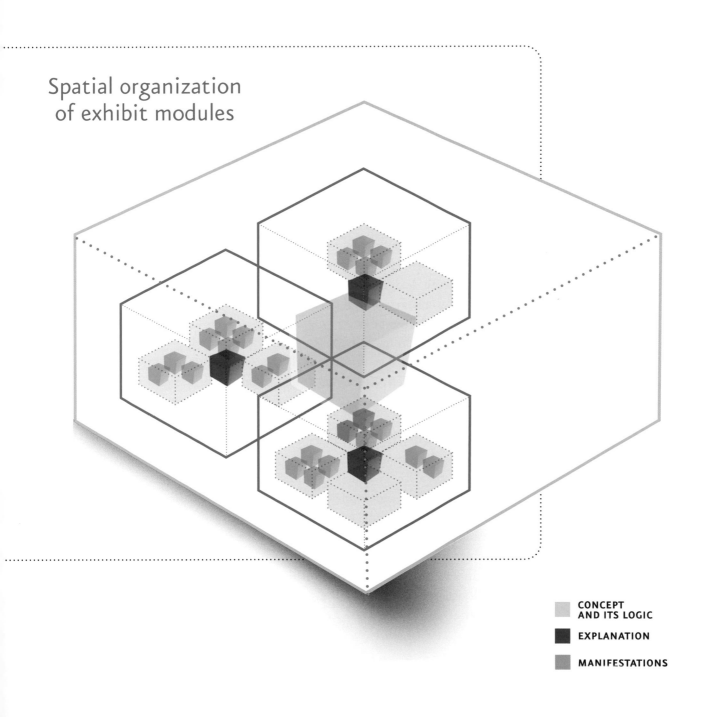

Spatial organization
of exhibit modules

CONCEPT
AND ITS LOGIC

EXPLANATION

MANIFESTATIONS

When designing sets, the following four basic guidelines are suggested:

1. The individual sets, as well as the entire space, need to be aesthetically appealing and provoke the imagination.
2. Each section of the story line, particularly if one is working with an entire museum or a gallery, needs to have a distinct design character.
3. Each "chapter" of the story line usually needs a visual icon that stands for the central idea. Using visual icons as metaphors for different topics is a very powerful visual communication device.
4. Different galleries and spaces need to have a different feel and appeal. As with music, varying rhythms, from dynamic to contemplative, add to a visitor's experience. As well, different members of the audience have different learning styles and respond to different approaches to design.

4·3·3   Design Phases

The design stage has three phases of development:

1. a **sketch design** phase,
2. a **preliminary design** phase, and
3. a **final design** phase.

A sketch design conveys the central idea and captures the overall atmosphere of a space. It also provides the basic spatial arrangement of the exhibit modules. The sketch design is sometimes accompanied by a model constructed to scale. These representations, however, will need to reflect budgetary possibilities. The sketch design and the scale model are usually presented to stakeholders and other evaluation groups.

The preliminary design conveys all the constructed elements of an exhibit and outlines the major choices that need to be made.

The final design renders all the installation details, accompanied by precise measurements and cost assessments, ready for fabrication considerations. If cost adjustments need to be made, it is easier and more efficient to make those adjustments as early as possible. Cost cutting in the final design phase is very difficult and usually not very successful in modifying the design. **Figure 4.3.3.a** explicates the three design phases and links them to the overall exhibit development process.

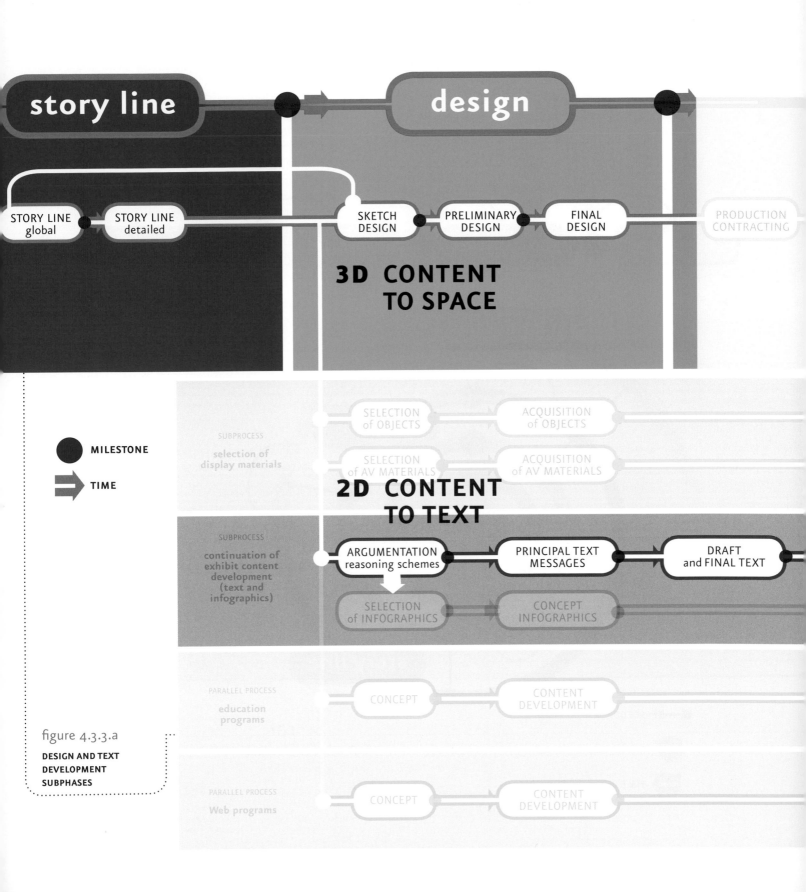

story line

design

| STORY LINE global | STORY LINE detailed | | SKETCH DESIGN | PRELIMINARY DESIGN | FINAL DESIGN | PRODUCTION CONTRACTING |

3D CONTENT TO SPACE

● **MILESTONE**

➡ **TIME**

SUBPROCESS
selection of display materials

| SELECTION of OBJECTS | ACQUISITION of OBJECTS |
| SELECTION of AV MATERIALS | ACQUISITION of AV MATERIALS |

2D CONTENT TO TEXT

SUBPROCESS
continuation of exhibit content development (text and infographics)

| ARGUMENTATION reasoning schemes | PRINCIPAL TEXT MESSAGES | DRAFT and FINAL TEXT |
| SELECTION of INFOGRAPHICS | CONCEPT INFOGRAPHICS | |

PARALLEL PROCESS
education programs

| CONCEPT | CONTENT DEVELOPMENT |

figure 4.3.3.a
DESIGN AND TEXT DEVELOPMENT SUBPHASES

PARALLEL PROCESS
Web programs

| CONCEPT | CONTENT DEVELOPMENT |

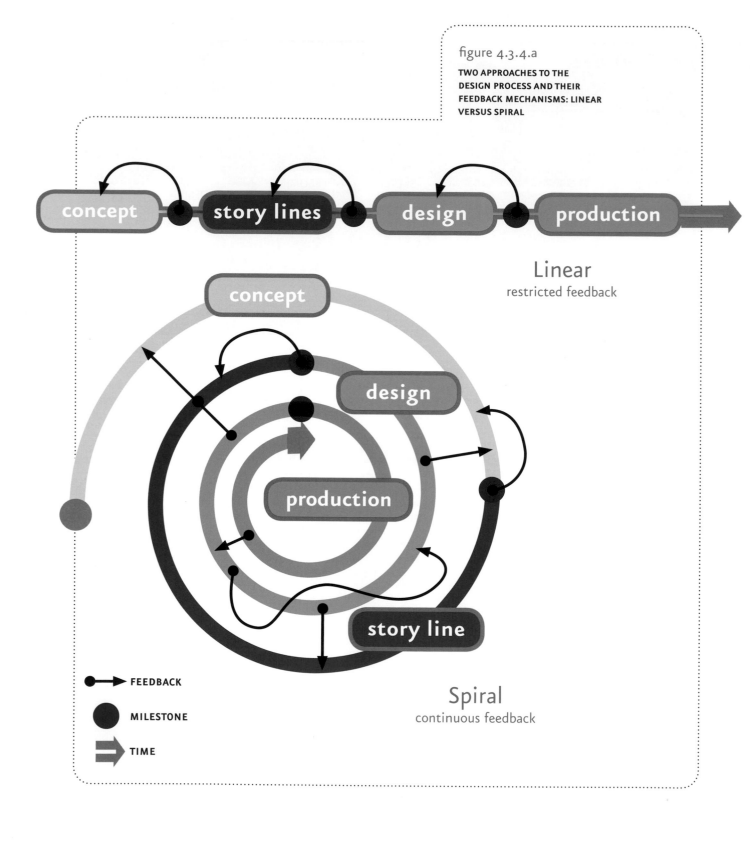

figure 4.3.4.a

TWO APPROACHES TO THE DESIGN PROCESS AND THEIR FEEDBACK MECHANISMS: LINEAR VERSUS SPIRAL

concept · story lines · design · production

Linear
restricted feedback

concept · design · production · story line

Spiral
continuous feedback

FEEDBACK

MILESTONE

TIME

While design phases are usually an established part of a museum's working methods, the way a particular institution approaches the process itself may be quite unique. For instance, Naturalis has a very strict, linear process. Upon completion and approval of one phase, there is no reconsideration of decisions already taken. In this process, each phase has its deliverables established. If disagreements occur, they have to be resolved within each phase. This process results in a very focused, efficient, and clearly defined approach, with outcomes determined for each stage.

Another museum could practice what might be described as a "spiral" process, one that is more open to change and might even result in a return to or reinvestigation of an earlier part or aspect of the process. For instance, during the preliminary design phase, changes could be made that would result in additional or more refined sketches, which would then need to be resubmitted for evaluation. The flexibility of this process provides room for additional creative input and corrections along the way, but it is more time-consuming. **Figure 4.3.4.a** represents a visualization of these two different design-development working methods, with feedback points indicated.

Design companies and designers have their strong points and weaknesses. Some, for example, excel in their knowledge and capacity to structure space, while others have highly imaginative approaches to exhibit scenography, defining a context and creating or accommodating audiovisual and atmospheric effects. A consideration of a designer's strong points or particular interests will be very important when choosing an individual or firm for needed tasks. For instance, when developing an overall master plan, the first type of designer or design group, with a particular sensitivity to the intellectual structuring of space, might be preferable to the second type, with a creative gift for designing sets and creating an appropriate atmosphere in each exhibit area.

In any case, if and when a museum may choose to work with an outside designer, the selection of designers has to be made on the basis of their affinities for the task, the subject matter, and the overall team dynamic. Design charettes, for example, allow an assessment of the working methods of different designers, their listening capacity, and inclination for teamwork. It is not unusual for a museum to consider many designers for a large master-planning project before short-listing or choosing only a few (for example, Naturalis interviewed thirty designers before selecting only seven). If an RFP is used to choose a designer, that document should carefully articulate the museum's content intentions.

In addition, when renovating an entire museum, there is a particular choice to be made between having a single designer direct the overall approach or assigning different galleries to different designers. The first approach may give a more unified overall appearance to the institution, while the second approach can provide a more diverse and tailored expression for each gallery and individual subject. If the second approach is adopted, then it is important to have a design director to harmonize the "look and feel" of the different galleries and spaces, as well as a strong content director to ensure that the messages remain consistent with the museum's overall intentions. The exhibit team members are discussed in the following section.

4.4 The Exhibit Development Team

To build a good exhibit requires the engagement and management of different disciplines and people, often over a period of years. This is likely to be particularly so when renovating or building a new museum.

To have a team work together as a unit for many years might be one of the most neglected aspects of the exhibit development process, as well as one of the most important. Like a sports team, an exhibit development team is more than the sum of its individual parts. Building such a team is not just about getting the best people, although the quality of individuals is very important. It is about the dynamics of the group, its joint vision and working style. It is also about finding the right people for the specific subject matter, with the presentation of the subject matter being influenced by the nature and quality or experience of the team members.

The key team members and their roles in the exhibit development process are the subject of the following section in *Mastering a Museum Plan*.

4.4.1 Exhibit Team Members and Their Roles

Certain exhibit teams may exist on an ongoing basis at any museum to monitor or generally oversee exhibit development activities or needs. For large-scale exhibit development, however, it is likely that a specific team (or teams) will be established when the project gets under way. The exhibit development team described below is usually central to the realization of a new installation.

The key members of an exhibit development team are usually: (1) the project manager/director, (2) the content director, (3) the art/design director, (4) the production manager, (5) the technology director/designer (electrical, multimedia, new media, etc.), and (6) the administrative/ finance coordinator. In addition to these members, a core exhibit team may have other regular players, including curators, interpretive planners (content developers), lighting designers, graphic designers, educators, marketing or fund-raising experts, and administrative support staff.

There are different ways of dividing the roles and responsibilities among the players on an exhibit team, as well as ways of structuring the team. However, some general circumstances seem to prevail. The project manager, the content director, the art/design director, and the production manager tend to be the principal players in the process of developing exhibits (see **fig. 4.4.1.a**). The project manager or content director often assumes the role of directing the project. The synergy and dynamics of such a group determine the working style of the entire team. The team members' ability to complement and inspire one another is essential.

The project manager/director, who is usually the leader of the project, organizes its meetings and drives its processes while reviewing the overall progress, timeline, and budget for the project. This position reports to the museum's director.

At first, the development of an installation must be driven by content, not by design or production. Thus, the project manager and the content director often share a background in the discipline to which the exhibit or the entire museum is devoted (although they may not be, or have been, curators), with an ability to communicate and popularize the subject, whatever it might be. Either the project manager or the content director will also lead the evaluation and stakeholder input processes.

The content director may be supported by one or more content developers, who are in charge of the creation and management of the project content. Their responsibility is to be in contact with content sources (including those in the museum); to select, organize, and present the relevant research findings, collection material, and other information; and to distinguish primary from secondary information. The role of content development is often combined with the duties of an interpretive planner (one or several, depending on the project), who will transform the content into written form. Curators, collection specialists, educators, and outside experts from different disciplines will provide essential information for the concept and overall content development, and its subsequent transformation into written texts. The graphic designer(s) should closely follow the work of the interpretive planner and, through collaboration, play a critical role in the visual presentation of the content, particularly when infographics are involved.

With innovative exhibitions and displays, the role of the art/design director becomes more prominent, although never to the point of overtaking the development of the content itself. The art/design director creates interpretive strategies and either serves as the principal designer or supervises the design work that leads to the two- and three-dimensional components that will deliver the developed concepts and content. This team member also provides an overall aesthetic for the museum's exhibits.

The production manager oversees the production process. It is essential that this key player is involved in the development of a project from the beginning, particularly because of the importance of value-engineering solutions to the design of the installation. This role also includes supervising the production of technical drawings for fabrication purposes and overseeing production meetings during the fabrication and installation stages. The production manager, together with the art/design director, also harmonizes and supervises the designers if the exhibits are being created by a number of independent design groups.

AV, multimedia, and lighting play a prominent role in the development of exhibits. Interactive devices and immersive environments have also become increasingly important for effective visitor experiences. As a consequence, another member of the core team is the technology director/designer, who plays a key role in determining the appropriate technologies for use in a project. Working with a lighting designer, the technology director/designer and the art/design director collaborate to realize a project's visual communication. These three designers need to have a compatible outlook and style in their aesthetic language and approach.

It should be pointed out that for smaller projects roles can be combined. Moreover, some individuals may possess more than one expertise, and this may somewhat influence the division of team tasks.

Administrative and financial support varies depending on the size of the project. For extensive installations or large renovations, a designated project office may be established under the overall direction of the project manager. This office can include an administrative/finance coordinator, usually a must in any large exhibit development process and often subdivided into separate positions, along with an administrative assistant. Their roles would include administrative tasks related to the management of contracts, budgets, and general administration.

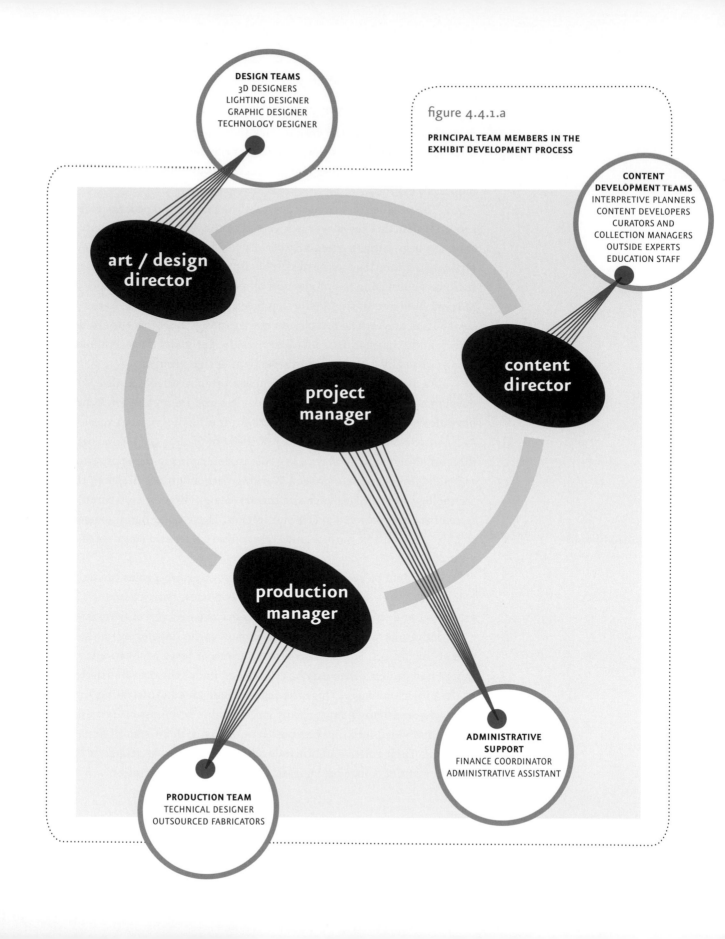

DESIGN TEAMS
3D DESIGNERS
LIGHTING DESIGNER
GRAPHIC DESIGNER
TECHNOLOGY DESIGNER

figure 4.4.1.a

**PRINCIPAL TEAM MEMBERS IN THE
EXHIBIT DEVELOPMENT PROCESS**

**CONTENT
DEVELOPMENT TEAMS**
INTERPRETIVE PLANNERS
CONTENT DEVELOPERS
CURATORS AND
COLLECTION MANAGERS
OUTSIDE EXPERTS
EDUCATION STAFF

art / design
director

project
manager

content
director

production
manager

**ADMINISTRATIVE
SUPPORT**
FINANCE COORDINATOR
ADMINISTRATIVE ASSISTANT

PRODUCTION TEAM
TECHNICAL DESIGNER
OUTSOURCED FABRICATORS

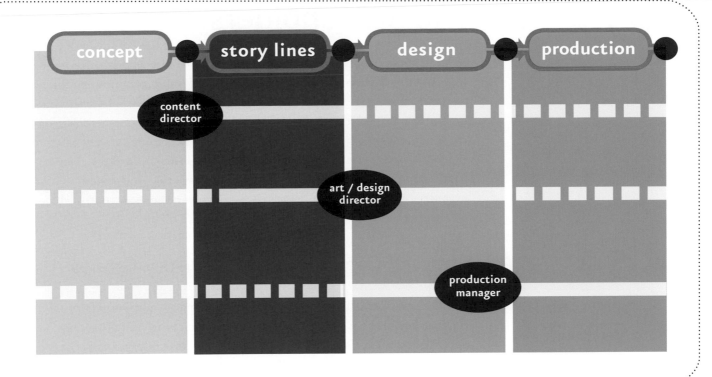

figure 4.4.1.b

**LEAD ROLES IN THE EXHIBIT
DEVELOPMENT PROCESS**

● MILESTONE

⇨ TIME

Over the course of the exhibition development process, the lead role changes as the project progresses. For instance, the content director often takes the lead during the concept and story line development phase and remains present and vigilant throughout the remaining stages.
The art/design director takes up the lead role through the design stages, with the production manager playing an increasingly important role.
In the production phase it is clearly the production manager who heads the process while keeping in close contact with both the art/design director and the content developer. The project manager/director oversees the entire process. **Figure 4.4.1.b** shows the lead roles during the exhibition development process.

During the development of a project, regular meetings will occur with the executive, marketing, and communications staffs, as well as the fund-raising department, in order to ensure that the essence of the project's intention, content, and progress is known and shared. Indeed, for large projects these departments may have regular members on the core development team.

4.5 The Stakeholders

In addition to the exhibit team, there are many others who are interested in or need or wish to contribute to the exhibit development process: for example, community or special-interest groups, schoolteachers, scientists, artists, members of the board of directors, and so on. Keeping a project on track while managing or responding to these many opinions is not easy.

To sustain the process and maintain the enthusiasm of all participants or contributors, it is essential to have the project well organized and transparent. Experience has proven the model outlined below effective.

4.5.1 Steering Committee and Advisory Groups

In the case of development of a major exhibition or extensive gallery renovations, there is usually a formal decision-making group that may have different names. In *Mastering a Museum Plan* it is referred to as the steering committee. This committee may consist of two or three board members, selected because of their special connection to the museum's exhibits or a particular project, the museum's director, chairs of advisory committees (see below), and representatives from the exhibit development teams, such as the project manager/director, content director, and/or the art/design director. This committee decides on all matters regarding the museum's exhibitions.

The steering committee often includes external representatives of all major stakeholder groups: academic disciplinary fields (from the sciences, arts, or humanities groups), various education services, the fields of marketing and fund-raising, museum peers, and community groups. Usually individuals, they speak on their own behalf and in the name of peers who may be members of one advisory group or another, created in conjunction with a project.

Advisory groups, each representing a different discipline or stakeholder group, are forums created in conjunction with a project for the examination and discussions of its particular aspects. Chairs of each advisory group are members of the steering committee.

The project manager/director, the content director, and the art/design director serve as representatives of a project and present it to

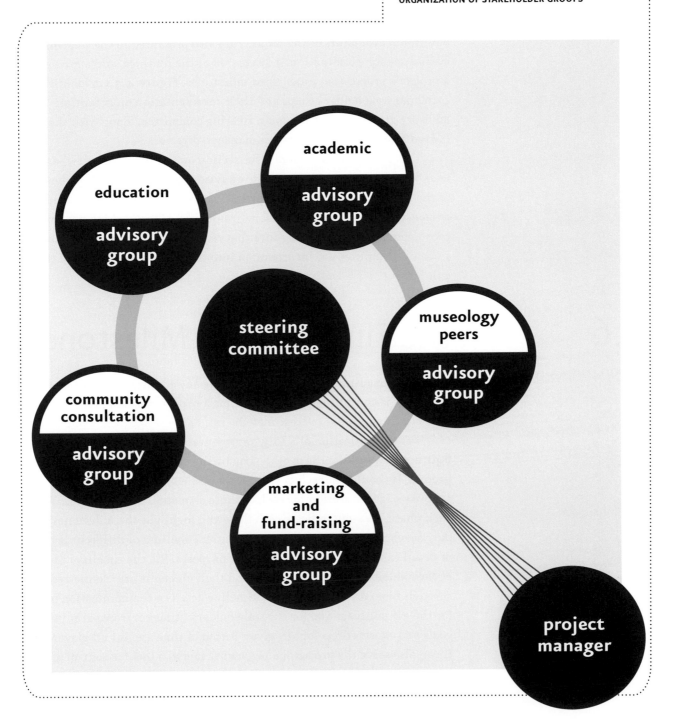

figure 4.5.1.a.
ORGANIZATION OF STAKEHOLDER GROUPS

any of the advisory groups and participate in their discussions. It is the role of these members of the core team to record and transmit suggestions or recommendations from advisory groups to the steering committee.

All evaluations carried out in different advisory groups, or by any additional evaluators of the project, are also presented to the steering committee for examination, a discussion of the findings, and approval of a project's progress, at established milestones. **Figure 4.5.1.a** identifies principal stakeholder groups and their representation on potential advisory groups around the main steering committee, along with the liaison role played by the project manager/director.

All milestone documents (see section on the timeline below) are usually presented to the appropriate advisory groups before they come to the steering committee for approval. The project manager/director is responsible for overseeing advisory group discussions, making note of recommendations, and being sure that recommendations approved by the steering committee are incorporated into the content and design of the exhibit.

4.6   The Timeline and Milestones

A detailed timeline for a project, including any connections to related activities, is an indispensable tool for mastering a museum plan. Its importance cannot be overestimated.

The organization of a fully representative timeline, as presented in **figure 4.6.a,** reflects the overall structuring of the exhibit development process. It should list each of the phases of work, indicate all their subphases, give duration for each of those elements, list the players for each phase, possibly indicate cash flow, and highlight the milestones (key developments and decision moments). Timelines of different levels of detail can be produced for different purposes. Via the timeline, each of the exhibit development phases and their elements are "connected" through time. A well-constructed timeline acts as a communication tool for the exhibit team and for the stakeholders. It makes transparent the goals and expectations for any given period of time and for all players. It can also serve the project management team as a tool for control of the processes, including their acceleration or deceleration. Changes to

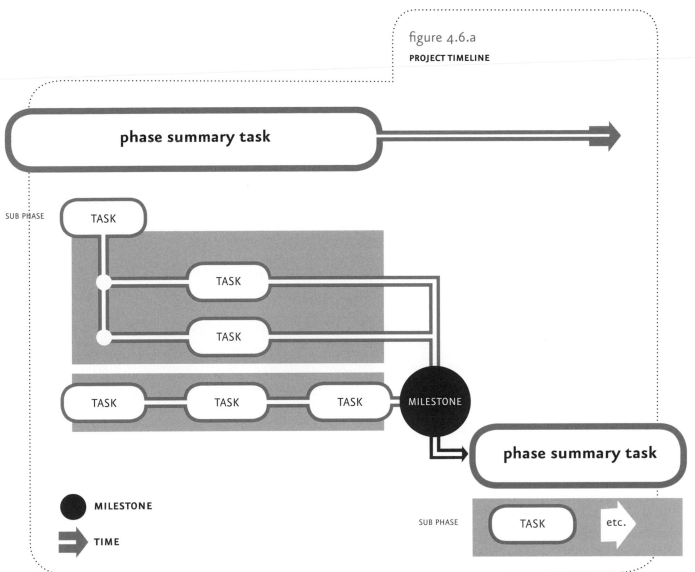

figure 4.6.a
PROJECT TIMELINE

timelines should be avoided (or made very rarely for exceptional reasons). This practice allows the pace of the project to be maintained.

Whichever project management software is used for the production of timelines, it is worthwhile investing in printers or plotters for very big paper sizes in order to produce detailed, clearly readable, large-scale timelines. These timelines need to be accessible to all team members at any moment throughout the process and are usually a centerpiece element in any project office or presentation. As well, reading and understanding complex timelines like those described here is a process that needs to be learned by the entire team.

figure 4.7.a

FINANCIAL INFORMATION
SYSTEM SPREADSHEETS

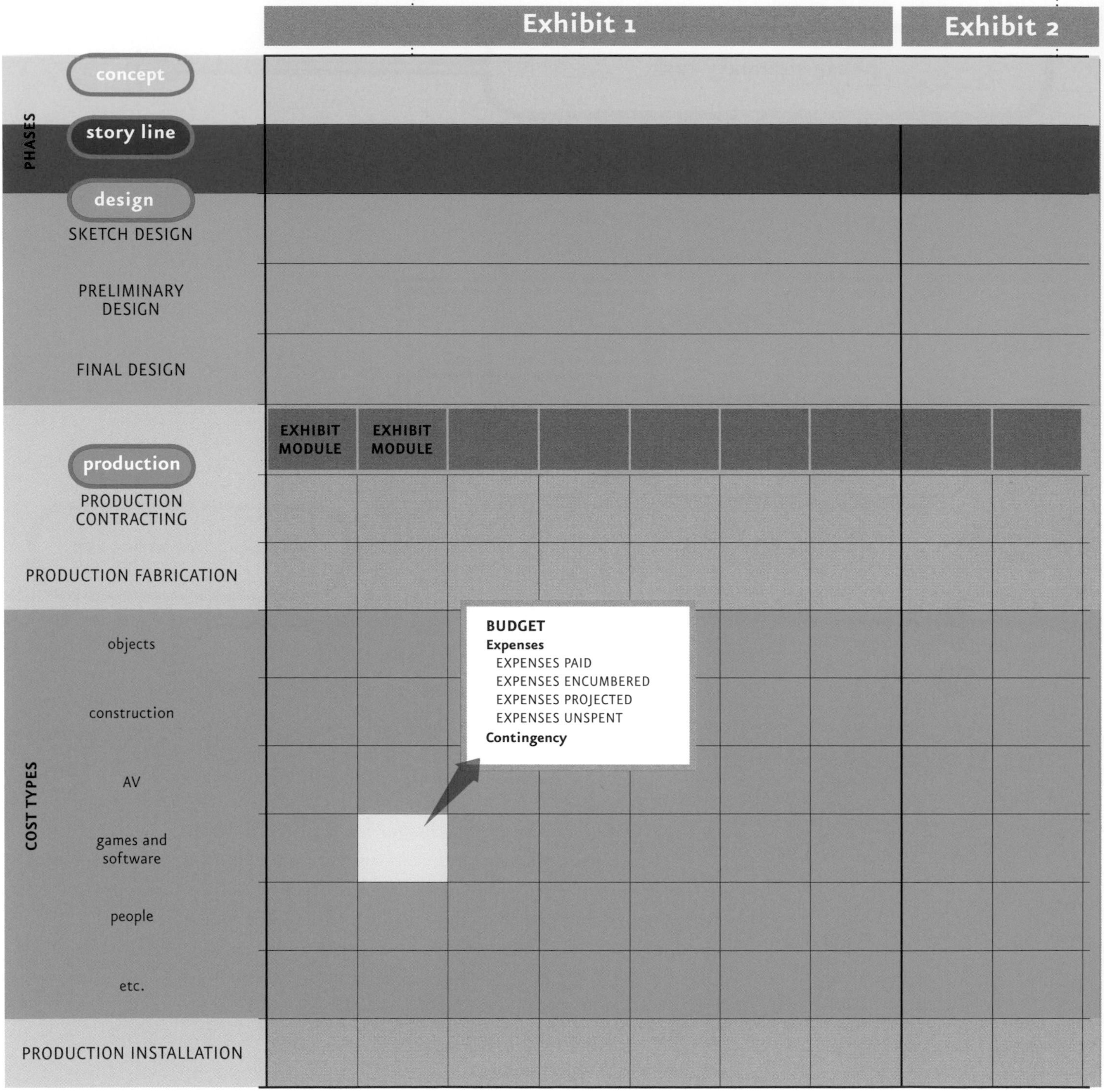

	Exhibit 1	Exhibit 2

PHASES

- concept
- story line
- design
  - SKETCH DESIGN
  - PRELIMINARY DESIGN
  - FINAL DESIGN
- production
  - PRODUCTION CONTRACTING
- PRODUCTION FABRICATION

EXHIBIT MODULE · EXHIBIT MODULE

COST TYPES

- objects
- construction
- AV
- games and software
- people
- etc.

PRODUCTION INSTALLATION

BUDGET
Expenses
  EXPENSES PAID
  EXPENSES ENCUMBERED
  EXPENSES PROJECTED
  EXPENSES UNSPENT
Contingency

Timelines also indicate milestones, formal decision-making moments in the working process. The milestones are characterized by a set of deliverables, and they mark the end of each phase (and/or subphase) of the development process. (See appendix for details.) As timeline components, at least their most significant items, are usually set at the beginning of a project's development, the milestones can be dated at least a year ahead, together with their deliverables. As they are moments when all decision makers need to agree on accomplishments to date, it is advisable to have milestones followed by a period that would accommodate inputs, corrections, and possible changes, particularly additions to the process that may result from consultations with the steering committee and/or advisory groups, etc. In this way deliverables can be corrected and adjusted.

Meetings are usually scheduled to mark milestones. These meetings are important and should be well prepared for and thoroughly organized. Decisions made during these meetings need to be clearly articulated when presented.

4.7 Budget

Whatever the budget, money often seems to fall short of a project's needs. Like attempts to make up lost time when a project has fallen behind schedule, cost-cutting measures in the later phases of a project are often unproductive. Therefore, it is important to share a few words here on proven ways to master the budget so that the exhibit development process is not rendered less meaningful as the end of a project is reached.

As soon as the concept development phase is concluded, a dedicated financial system needs to be put in place, guided by an experienced finance coordinator who is a member of the exhibit development team. It is highly unlikely that a museum's general finance administration has the necessary time and capacity to master a large capital project such as a gallery renovation. Therefore, it is important to plan for and include a finance coordinator on the project team and to invest the time to develop an effective financial information system.

The financial information system template presented in **figure 4.7.a,** is essentially a fine-grained spreadsheet that goes into greater detail and indicates links that may not have always been part of a traditional budget tracking system. The columns list the exhibits and their modules while the rows list the phases of the project with their specific tasks, divided into an expense for each type of exhibit component. Thus, this spreadsheet is closely related to the timeline and its phases, as well as to the actual exhibit modules. In this elaborated version of a spreadsheet, each of the cells provides a series of budgetary details listing expenses for paid, encumbered, projected, and unspent expanses for each component of the exhibit.

Framework budgets, or projected budgets, for all exhibits need to be developed beforehand. In practice, some 5 percent of the total budget is usually dedicated to concept and story line development; 15 to 20 percent to design; 65 to 70 percent to production. The remaining 10 percent should be set aside for post-opening adjustments.

The development of a detailed framework budget includes assigning percentage costs for each exhibit and for each of its modules. This detailed budget allows the project manager, production manager, and financial coordinator to monitor and control expenditures. The best practice is never to allow any of the individual expenses to surpass the allotted amounts. In this way, certain amounts are kept aside for unexpected expenses, which do arise in large and complex projects. In order to best understand and control the budget, it is advisable to keep track of projected, encumbered, paid, and unspent expenses for each item.

The advantages of investing in the management of budgets—as well as time to monitor them properly throughout the project, particularly during the content-to-design phase—cannot be overstressed.

Conclusion

TODAY AN EFFECTIVE EXHIBITION AT ANY MUSEUM
is dependent on the processes that have led to its
realization. This includes the structuring of the
museum's available intellectual and collection
resources and following or using certain key
planning strategies. The methodology for mastering
a museum plan, emphasized here, is essential for
the development of an entire museum installation
or reinstallation, as well as for a single exhibit. This
is especially true for large, encyclopedic museums
with diverse collections and resident expertise. As
well, the system outlined in *Mastering a Museum Plan*
is applicable to museums in general and can be used
not only for their exhibits but also to help guide the
development of other program activities.

Regardless of the circumstances, a museum
must recognizes that a master-planning process
involves a close-knit, interrelated system requiring
both broad and precise management protocols
to achieve the desired results. The principal
characteristics of the methodology presented in
Mastering a Museum Plan involve the close integration
of the various aspects of the development process,
including the concept, the content, the design,
the participants, the timeline, and the budget. In
addition, such an approach is invaluable for making
an exhibit master plan transparent, for managing
the expectations of all involved, and

for communicating the project to the museum's
entire staff and its stakeholders.

Exhibits resulting from the application of the
methodology described in *Mastering a Museum Plan*
may be extremely varied. The quality and diversity
of a museum's thinking about itself, its collections,
and its role; the imagination of its team members;
the taste for innovation and originality expressed by
its stakeholders; and the amount of time and money
available, for example, all contribute to the final
exhibit project and the experiences it can provide.

Finally, it is important to remember that
visitors also contribute to the result, bringing their
own knowledge, tastes, interests, and inclinations.
Thus, the methodology presented in *Mastering a
Museum Plan* does not guarantee a successful public
experience. It will, however, help a museum to
clearly articulate its message and to organize its
exhibit development activity in a much more
orderly, professional, and respectful fashion; to
avoid crisis management; and to prevent a loss of
the organizers' energy and resources.

Needless to say, the strategies presented here
are not the only ones that a museum may use while
developing an exhibit. These particular elements
have been emphasized, however, because practice
has shown that they are essential to mastering a
museum plan.

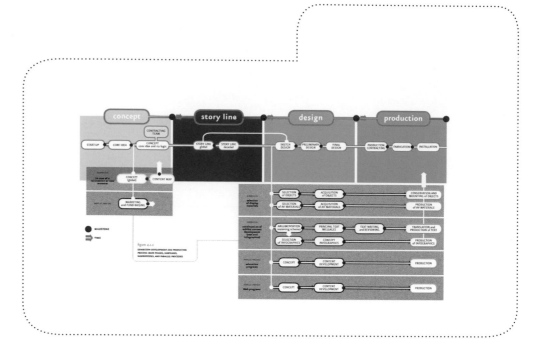

Appendix: Overall Exhibit Development and Production Process and Its Deliverables

This appendix outlines the four main phases of the overall exhibit development process and their subphases, subprocesses, and parallel processes as well as opening and post-opening exhibit maintenance. It indicates which team member has the lead role during a particular phase or process and the deliverable(s) or milestone(s) associated with that phase or process. It corresponds to **figure 4.1.c** in the main text of *Mastering a Museum Plan*.

PHASE	DESCRIPTION	DELIVERABLE
	# The Main Process: Exhibit Development and Production Process	
Concept Phase	The concept phase takes the museum through the process of considering and fully defining a central or core idea for an installation or display.	A concept that defines the core idea and its logic.
Start-up	The start-up phase sets out the basic terms of the proposed project and its objectives.	At the end of this start-up phase (with its subphases), deliverables include a project description, preliminary timeline, initial organizational chart, and budget estimate.
Initial idea(s)	What is the idea (or ideas) for a projected display or installation, and how well does it meet the expectations of the museum and its main stakeholders, both inside and outside the museum (including the museum's audiences)? How does it fit within the museum's philosophy and activities? How does it relate to the other "players" and the competitive environment? Lead role: content director.	A report that includes a presentation of the proposed idea and how it serves the expectations of the stakeholders and the museum's field of activities and research. An analysis of the museum's "market" and competitive position is part of the deliverable.
Preliminary budget assessment	What is the range of prices per square foot/meter for a project of this size and substance? What is the estimated or potential overall budget for the project? What are some key budget figures on items such as the acquisition of specific objects for display, building renovations, new technologies, travel expenses to see relevant installations at other museums, etc. Lead role: project manager.	An overview of budget expectations and prices, in a generalized way, with some detailed figures on specific project items of relevance to the museum.
Preliminary ideas on project team(s)	What team(s) should be in place to run a project and, possibly, to oversee it? Does the existing museum staff have the capacity to undertake the entire project or just specific parts of it? Who are the most significant stakeholders and how should they be represented on the teams established in conjunction with a project? Who needs to be on an overall exhibition steering committee (whether one already exists or not)? Lead role: project manager.	An outline of the work process, which consists of an initial organizational chart, including museum and stakeholder representation at various levels of activity and responsibility, and the overall decision-making process. Selection and contracting of project team(s).
Process description and preliminary timeline	A description of the work process (for example, as outlined in this appendix), adjusted to institutional conditions and translated into a preliminary timeline with milestones. Lead role: project manager.	A generalized but detailed timeline, including all phases, milestones, and deliverables.

PHASE	DESCRIPTION	DELIVERABLE
Core idea	The core idea reflects the essence of the new or renovated museum, and/or new exhibit. That idea must be consistent with the museum's vision, mission, values, intellectual activities, audience, etc. Lead role: content director.	A short description (perhaps only one paragraph) that outlines the essential core idea and contents of a forthcoming project and how it relates to the museum and its stakeholders, staff capacity, market, budget, etc.
Concept	The concept is an elaboration of the core idea, now including the logic of its underlying structure. Often this description of the concept involves broad research into the literature on the topic and discussion with experts. Stakeholders and visitors can be surveyed for their reactions to the proposed concept. The concept becomes the basis for the project's future development. Lead role: content director.	A report explaining the core idea and its underlying logic. It is represented in a visual, a schematic drawing. A front-end visitor evaluation may be conducted at this point; results may be included in the report.
Story Line Phase	This phase describes, in depth, the narrative or story line of the chosen concept. In addition to detailing the story line itself, this phase gathers examples, ideas, and options for transmitting the story.	Detailed project story line(s).
Global story line	The function of the global story line is to outline the content of the project and to serve as a communication piece to inform all project teams, the designer, other stakeholders, future evaluation activities, etc. Therefore, it restricts itself to the major components, up to the second or third level of detailing. It consists of schemes, text, and drawings, and is the starting point for the sketch design (see Design Phase, below). Lead role: content director.	A content map, thematic structure, and written table consisting of all content components to be considered, listed, and numbered, with an outline showing how they relate to the concept—and also the preliminary ideas on the form and content of the presentation.
Detailed story line	The detailed story line describes, in depth, all facts and figures related or relevant to the components concerned, up to the most detailed level. The project contents are strictly organized in a gridlike format that expresses the logical structure of the concept and serves as the reference for all involved in the development or approval of the project. As this is a major undertaking, it may end up as a book on the subject. Lead role: content developer and/or interpretive planner.	A substantial and detailed manuscript discussing the project's content, strictly organized to reflect any modular aspects of the elaborated concept itself.
Design Phase	It is in this phase that project content meets design, and these essential aspects of a project must connect logically and visually. This very critical phase is divided into three distinct steps to guarantee an outcome that meets stated expectations.	The design phase, in the end, delivers a final, overall design for the production of the project.
Sketch design	In the sketch design stage, the major concern is to connect content and space and deliver "the big idea" of the design approach, as well as the voice and tone of the installation. Sketches developed during this stage are used in further visitor surveys and become part of the decision-making process. Lead role: design director.	An overview (bird's-eye) sketch or sketches, some detailing of major aspects of the exhibit, a floor plan, a description of the style of the installation, possibly a three-dimensional scale model, some preliminary calculations, and a front-end visitor survey.

PHASE	DESCRIPTION	DELIVERABLE
Preliminary design	The chosen sketch design is now detailed to include all design elements, including objects, audiovisual presentations, interpretive components, etc. In addition to descriptive drawings for all content components determined to date, there is an outline of all necessary technical feasibility and prototyping studies and budget calculations. Lead role: design director.	An extensive sketchbook, a possible scale model, or individual component prototypes, as well as dimensions and cost calculation sheets. Another front-end visitor survey on specific points may be included if design clarification is needed.
Final design	The aim is to detail all design elements for production drawings. Corrections to costs, technical features, objects selected, etc., are indicated, but within the boundaries of the earlier proposals. The final design should represent a clear understanding of all aspects of the design. Lead role: production manager.	A "book" consisting of all design drawings and calculations, including visitor responses to the concept and design for it.
Production Phase	The production phase involves fabrication and installation of the exhibits.	Fabricated and installed exhibit.
Production contracting	This subphase describes various aspects of the production process when developing an installation, including the outsourcing of fabrication. This is a phase, with several subphases, in which contractors are determined, prices are set, and timelines and calculations are, if necessary, adapted. This part of the process might also be an integral part of the work of the design company if design and fabrication are combined in a "turnkey" installation.	A list of needs, the drafting of tender documents, the selection of possible contractors, the detailing of production data, etc. The final deliverables are the contract and the selected contractors.
Selection procedure	The search for suitable production companies as well as acceptable pricing (including specific costing for items such as showcases) requires considerable time. Reputable and experienced contractors represent a huge advantage. Lead role: production manager.	A short list of contractors (suppliers and fabricators) and related needs.
Tendering	The tendering process will likely follow local procedures, which might vary from country to country. It is important for the museum to work up a detailed tender-request package and to have it well distributed at the start of this procedure. Lead role: project manager.	At the outset of this process, a tender request and package of drawings and specifications, with a clear articulation of terms and their characteristics, as well as other conditions.
Selection, additional negotiations, contract	Once the bids are received, clarifications may be needed on prices, areas where the responsibilities of two or more contractors meet or overlap (electrical wiring, audiovisuals, and information and communication technology, for example), technical descriptions, guarantees and support, etc. Additional time may be needed for recalculating and/or amending the actual contracts. The selection of contractor(s) should not be rushed. Lead role: project manager.	A set of contracts with project contractor(s) and the establishment of work protocol.
Fabrication	Fabrication leads to the creation of various components ready for the installation of a project's contents. This phase, in particular, may have interwoven parts from different contractors, which sometimes continues during the actual installation.	Creation of a project's various contents.
Preparation of fabrication	The initial preparation results in (a) working drawings, (b) a detailed production plan, (c) orders for materials (remember to adequately consider delivery times/delays), and (d, optional) contracts with small or specialized subcontract parties. Lead role: production manager.	Sets of drawings, a list of subcontractors, and a timeline that gathers together all time-based flows.

PHASE	DESCRIPTION	DELIVERABLE
Actual fabrication (inside and outside museum)	A considerable amount of time is likely to be spent by fabricators, suppliers, internal suppliers, third parties, etc., to create project contents, which may include the components of an overall gallery setting, individual object display components, audiovisual settings, graphic displays, printed materials, etc. It must also include time for the conservation, preparation, and mounting of objects for display. Lead role: production manager.	Ready-made or fully prepared, and approved, installation components.
Installation	This stage involves the installation of all project contents.	The installed and fully functional exhibit.
Gallery preparation	The preparation of the gallery (galleries) for installation consists of cleaning, refurbishment, adding or improving electrical and information technology installations, etc. Lead role: production manager.	An empty gallery space, with the needed installation equipment and materials at hand.
Transport and storage	In a parallel process, the transportation and storage of all installation content materials and equipment need to be considered as well as the possible move of objects from a preparation facility to the galleries. This phase may be outsourced or included in the fabricators' responsibilities. Lead role: production manager.	A table indicating transportation services being used, storage locations (on- or off-site), downloading and installation equipment required, and the plan for downloading components.
Installation (in gallery)	The actual assembly of a project's content components and their installation can be a very labor-intensive part of the overall process for a project. Scheduling of the installation is often difficult, and long working hours can be expected. Partial delivery of the overall installation should be avoided. Lead role: production manager.	A completely installed exhibit, ready for testing and approval.
Testing and delivery or completion	Testing, remedial evaluation, and fine-tuning of the installation are the focus of this phase. It is not unusual to have this phase extended until after the official opening, as often some problems become apparent only after initial use of the exhibit. Lead role: production manager.	The museum's formal acceptance of the installation.
Opening	The opening marks the formal end of the exhibit development process and the starting point for the presentation and maintenance of the installation. In practice, however, there is often an overlap, when the formal delivery has not yet been accepted by the museum and/or its maintenance has not been transferred from exhibit fabricators to the maintenance staff. Lead role: project manager.	
Maintenance	The maintenance of an installation is also part of the production planning procedure, although often not incorporated. There must be a consideration of, and budget for, the actual "wear and tear" on a new installation, and how to deal with its maintenance in financial terms as well as staffing, training, documentation, and responsibility.	The project continues to operate as expected.
Maintenance, adjustments, and adaptations	A set of maintenance instructions and documentation is needed for maintenance staff and other internal services. The technical documentation is part of the contract(s) with the fabricator(s). Of equal importance is a procedure for handling or dealing with adjustments and adaptations that may be required as a result of technical, design, or other malfunctions. Lead role: production manager.	The documentation for maintenance staff and instructions for other technical staff, including procedures for dealing with modifications (needed or desired).
Summative surveys and adaptations	Summative visitor evaluations, peer evaluation, and exhibit development staff evaluation are carried out during this phase along with, if needed, the installation adjustments that come out of the surveys or that are otherwise identified. Lead role: project manager.	The results of all surveys and the list of proposed changes and adaptations.

PHASE	DESCRIPTION	DELIVERABLE
Deinstallation and reuse	The actual dismantling of an exhibit, including the possible reuse of infrastructure materials and/or the renovation of display items, if necessary. Lead role: project manager.	A preliminary list of components of the exhibit, their "owners" (including the museum itself) and how/where to return items, as necessary, after closing of the exhibit.
Archiving	Who is going to store what? Selected deliverables (display objects, infrastructure material, etc.) and installation documentation (e.g., video or photographic records), as well as all adjustments and maintenance experiences during the installation, need to be cataloged and stored in such a way that retrieving a record of the installation, or the physical components of it, is fast and easy. For example, the need for retrieving images and texts years after an opening is often underestimated. As archiving is necessary and important throughout the process, it is best to prepare for it at the start of the project. Lead role: project manager.	The archive of the exhibit development, production, and installation.

Subprocesses

PHASE	DESCRIPTION	DELIVERABLE
	Given the function or intention of the following three subphases within the overall development phase itself (i.e., from the development of the core idea through the design stage), these subprocesses are presented at a slightly more general level.	See below.
Subprocess: Concept Development for an Extended or Entire Museum Installation	This subprocess considers how an idea for an overall installation of a renovated or new museum must be developed so as to connect the individual parts of an idea logically and deliver a structured content that can also be connected to the floor plan of the museum's galleries.	
Concept	The phase is in essence an elaboration of the single exhibit concept phase, but it includes the concept for the entire museum (the core idea in its major components), structured in a logical and visually consistent proposal. In this subphase, the proposal is restricted to the major components as it needs to correspond to the architectural spaces of the overall building facility. Lead role: content director.	The concept for the entire space/museum (core idea and its logic structure), represented in a schematic drawing with sketches that capture the style of each part of the installation. A front-end visitor evaluation can be part of this report.
Content Map	As most museums have an existing building, the content map for a new or renovated collection presentation would need to be "laid over" the existing museum floor plan. It is important to maintain the logic/consistency of the core idea in the content map. The exhibits should stay on the same level of abstraction and connect logically to support the overarching core idea, as the museum should strive for a logical structure of its entire installation. Lead role: content director.	A content map that lays out the exhibit floor plan of the museum, showing the designated themed galleries and, eventually, a suggested visitors' path.

PHASE	DESCRIPTION	DELIVERABLE
Subprocess: Selection of the Display Materials	The story lines lead to the consideration of the ways and means to communicate those stories. The visual carriers of the story line can be the objects themselves, audiovisual materials, infographics, texts, etc. The selection of objects, as well as the development of audiovisuals (including interactive software) for installation, is a task not to be underestimated. Often it requires more time than originally allotted to it and is a challenging logistical procedure. These tasks therefore require separate phases and planning.	
General		
Selection of objects	Before the exhibition development process starts, there is likely to be an understanding on the part of the museum as to its key collection objects for display (the "masterpieces" of the museum). However, many objects have to be chosen or confirmed while work proceeds on the story line and the design. The desired objects, as well as the display characteristics they should have, are set out in "wish lists" indicating their relative importance and possible alternatives. Lead role: content director.	An extensive database consisting of a list of objects (including alternatives), their material and display characteristics, their need for conservation and preparation and mounting, the cost of these procedures, and the exhibit module to which they belong.
Acquisition or loan of additional objects	If necessary or desirable for a particular display, objects need to be acquired or borrowed. Locating these objects and negotiating the terms of their use is not an easy task and requires considerable time. Keeping track of the preparation status (conservation, mounting, etc.) necessary for such objects, as well as the budget required, is also essential. Lead role: project manager.	An updated database of all objects (including status, etc.) anticipated for installation.
Conservation and mounting of objects	As most objects need additional treatment, their conservation, preparation, and mounting need to be done by staff or outsourced. For an installation of an entire museum, thousands of objects need to be prepared. This may take years of work. Lead role: production manager.	A database that includes the tracking information on the location and treatment (including the duration and status of the treatment) for all objects. It also needs to include the "production" flow chart for the objects and the protocols for their move, storage, and security.
Selection of AV	Choosing the kind of audiovisual presentations, photographs, film sequences, etc. to be used should be undertaken in relation to the stories and the choice of objects as they have to complement one another in their capacity to transmit the story line. Lead role: content director	As with the objects, the deliverable is a database listing all wanted images (moving or still) and their contents, including alternatives, and an indication of the display module to which they belong.

PHASE	DESCRIPTION	DELIVERABLE
Acquisition of audiovisuals	As is the case with the objects, the process of acquiring audiovisuals, or finding suitable alternatives, is costly and time-consuming and needs considerable attention. Lead role: AV director.	A timeline, including the steps to be taken to acquire desired materials, as well as a detailed database tracking system.
Production of AV material	Photographs, film/video footage(s), and/or audio recordings may have to be made specifically for the installation in order to illustrate or present a certain component of a story line. The process of shooting, editing, and producing such material is costly and time-consuming and has to be done in parallel with fabrication of sets. Lead role: AV director.	Stills, video, or sound material ready for installation.
Subprocess: Continuation of Exhibit Content Development	Content development will be reflected in the overall design of an installation, including the organization of collection objects and interpretive support material such as text panels, audiovisual presentations, labels, etc. Texts and infographics are added to explain a display using either a narrative or visuals. Although text panels may seem too "didactic" and inconsistent with the emphasis on the visual experience in museum presentations, they are still a major contributor to conscious information transfer. Lead role: content director.	Texts and infographics to augment a display.
Argumentation (reasoning schemes)	Reasoning schemes are created to check the validity of the scientific construct, and its logic, with scientific experts. They are a drawn up as a set of arguments, constructed in a logical, structured schema. It is sometimes also (informally) called the "bullet schema." The reason for undertaking this argumentation is to facilitate subsequent text writing and to check the content of the texts and their logic with experts. Lead role: content director.	A reasoning schema for each and every module in the story line. If correct and approved, they serve as input for the next phase in this subprocess (text messages, below).
Principal text messages	In each and every module of the story line, the text components are presented so as to distinguish their importance and, as well, to anticipate different levels of "learning" interest that a visitor may have. These text messages (or "content parts") serve as building blocks for text writing. The clusters of text components are also developed with the school curriculum and other target groups in mind. Lead role: content director.	An extended document consisting of all text messages.
Text writing and reviewing	The draft texts are read and reread by a review group. Different members may be assigned different aspects of the text (its logic, attractiveness, comprehensibility, terminology, appropriate word use, etc.). Some visitor testing of these texts should also be included. Lead role: content director.	A collection of finished texts, neatly organized in large batches by modules.
Translation and production	When necessary, the translation (and checking) of texts flows into the actual production of the graphic panels. All texts should undergo copyediting before they go into print. This phase is notorious for mistakes, misunderstandings, last-minute adaptations, etc. A well-organized flow of full-scale mock-ups will help reduce the level of stress and error. Lead role: production manager.	A complete set of copy proofs (to be checked) and a finished set of panels for production.

PHASE	DESCRIPTION	DELIVERABLE
Selection of infographics	An infographic is a visual presentation that is closely connected to, or even substitutes for, text. In cases where drawing may explain certain processes better than words, infographics are needed. One challenge, however, lies in the time-consuming and relatively expensive production of infographics. Animations are considered "moving infographics" and are part of this phase. Decision-making on whether a certain form of information is to be explained by an infographic or text leads to a wish list. Ideally this is detailed with existing examples. Some preliminary cost calculations are also included in this phase. Lead role: content director.	A list or database of possible infographics.
Concept infographics	Each infographic is defined in terms of its location in the exhibit as well as its own intrinsic structure and principal message. This information is accompanied by illustrations showing the process and perhaps highlighting certain components. The infographics are to be checked with experts to ensure that they match the argumentation for the concept being given a graphic representation. At the same time, a style sheet is made under the direction of the design director to define the graphic style, use of colors, etc. Lead role: content director.	A more detailed overview of all infographics to be produced, as well as their principal messages and, separately, a generalized example/style sheet for all infographics.
Production of infographics	The actual production of infographics by illustrators takes time. Their production also needs to be monitored carefully. The process will include reviewing the graphics and their texts, as well as any other texts in the same display. When outsourcing this task, the choice of illustrators or designers who can work quickly, easily incorporate changes, and deliver illustrations built up in digital layers (which allows components to be used individually) is an important concern, as is the cost per illustration. Lead role: production manager.	At the beginning of this subprocess, the deliverable is a detailed timeline, including ample time for corrections. The end result consists of the actual drawings, which will flow into the overall production of the various exhibit modules.

PHASE	DESCRIPTION	DELIVERABLE
	## Parallel Processes	
General	All the content information gathered and organized for an installation is put to further use in the museum. For example, it can be used for the development of education programs and outreach material, Web theme content, lectures, etc. A modern museum is an information generalist within its knowledge domain and, given its public status, should distribute information not only through its exhibits but through other outlets as well. Two possible outlets—education programs and Web programs—are presented here. The development of the parallel processes follows its own protocols, which are not a subject of this publication.	Complementary uses (see examples below) of information and input gathered by the museum during an installation development process.
	## Parallel Process: Education Programs	
General	The production of accompanying educational programs requires its own development process and production system. Education programs and outreach material are based on the story line of the exhibit and take into account all exhibit elements. There is a mutual influence, as the exhibit includes input in the form of team representation, information, needs, etc., from education staff.	Educational programs that resonate with the concept and execution of the exhibit.
	## Parallel Process: Web Programs	
General	Alongside each exhibit, extensive Web programming can draw upon the information and graphics developed for an installation project. In effect, it can reuse or adapt the exhibit content, story line, texts, infographics, and audiovisuals, as well as the entire design style of the installation. Its content and production need to be adjusted to the Web medium.	Web programs that resonate with the concept and the execution of the exhibit.
	## Parallel Process: Marketing and Fund-raising	
General	The strategic positioning of the museum within its knowledge domain, and within the realm of related or comparable institutions, is important. It is essential, therefore, from the beginning of the development process that the marketing group is represented on the project team and on the steering committee and is always present to understand and possibly influence decisions being made. The same can also be said for the department responsible for fund-raising. It is important that marketing and fund-raising expectations or objectives are clearly articulated in written form. It can be very disruptive if plans or goals change during the development process because of changes in the museum's approach to its markets or possible funding sources after a project is under way.	A set of expectations or criteria, as well as strategic considerations and objectives, for marketing a project and for the development of financial support for it.